CRESCENT MOON RISING

The Islamic Invasion of America

The Sons of Rebellion

ED DECKER

LAMP POST
publishers

CRESCENT MOON RISING
The Islamic Invasion of America
by Ed Decker

Copyright © 2017 by J. Edward Decker. All rights reserved.

www.saintsalive.com

Unless otherwise noted, all scripture quotations are from THE HOLY BIBLE, NEW INTERNATIONAL VERSION®, NIV®. Copyright © 1973, 1978, 1984 by Biblica US, Inc.®. Used by permission.

Scripture quotations marked (NKJV) are taken from the New King James Version. Copyright © 1982 by Thomas Nelson, Inc. All rights reserved. Used by permission.

Without limiting the rights under copyright reserved above, no part of this publication – whether in printed or ebook format, or any other published derivation – may be reproduced, stored in or introduced into a retrieval system, or transmitted, in any form or by any means (electronic, mechanical, photocopying, recording or otherwise), without the prior written permission of the publisher.

The scanning, uploading, and distribution of this book via the Internet or via any other means without the permission of the publisher is illegal and punishable by law. Please purchase only authorized electronic editions and do not participate in or encourage electronic piracy of copyrightable materials.

Published by:

www.lamppostpublishers.com

Trade Paperback: ISBN-13 # 978-1-60039-240-5
ebook: ISBN-13 # 978-1-60039-745-5

*And he will be a wild man;
his hand will be against every man
and every man's hand against him.*
                              Genesis 16:12 KJV

CONTENTS

Foreword .... *vii*

Introduction .... *ix*

1. Opening the Gates to the Enemy 3
2. Has America Lost its Soul? 9
3. How Did We Become an Anti-Christ Nation? 13
4. Remembering September 11, 2001 19
5. If Just a Tenth of a Tenth of a Tenth 23
6. Accidentally Stirring the Wrath of Islam 27
7. The Faith of Mohammed 31
8. A Word to the Muslim Reader 33
9. Islam Across the World 37
10. A People Cut Off from the Christian World View 41
11. A Seventh Century People in a Twenty-First Century World 45
12. The Women of Islam 49
13. The Gods of the Seventh Century 61
14. The New Age of Islam Begins 65
15. Sharia Law 67
16. The Six Beliefs of Islam 73
17. The Five Pillars of Islam 75
18. Islam and Christianity Compared 77
19. Is Allah the God of Abraham, Isaac, and Jacob? 85
20. Islam and Freemasonry 89
21. It's a Mystery to Me 97
22. Jesus and Mohammed 101
23. The Holy Jihad – A Way of Life and Death 103
24. A Holy War Fought to the Death without Compromise 107
25. Terrorism is All About Islam 113
26. Is the Jihad Really the Core of Islamic Doctrine? 117
27. Beyond the Jihad: Apocalyptic Islam 125
28. The Glory of Martyrdom – A Holy Death 127
29. The Words of Winston Churchill 129
30. Finally, Brethren, Some Words of Sound Advice 131
31. Witnessing to Muslims 133
32. A Call to Arms 145

Foreword

Upon receiving Ed Decker's new book, *Crescent Moon Rising*, I was extremely impressed with both the depth and the breadth of his coverage on this very pertinent topic. Having read numerous secular and Christian books on the topic of Islam, I don't believe I have seen one as thoughtful and thorough as this book.

Decker's newest work is a clarion call to both Christians and concerned Americans regarding the beliefs and actual intent set forth by Muhammad in the seventh century.

The reader will understand that behind the façade that seeks to portray Islam as a "religion of peace," there is but one motive that it's ancient founder, and now 21st century adherents, ascribe to: complete religious and political domination of the non-Muslim infidel wherever they may be.

I suggest the Western world must quickly wake up to that truth before it is too late.

May Jehovah God use this book as a tool to do just that in the lives of all Americans!

Eric Barger
Take A Stand! Ministries
www.ericbarger.com

Find Eric Barger in conferences and churches across North America at www.ericbarger.com and weekly on Take A Stand! TV

Introduction

Islam is a critical issue and a major threat to the sovereignty of our nation, and to the whole world. It is an evil, demonic, and violent system, coming into America in waves; through doors held wide open by our own leaders in the government, in our education system, and in the private sector.

This is a bold charge, but its truth is evident. During the 2017 Islamic month of Ramadan, spanning from May 27 to June 9, there were forty-two Muslim terrorist attacks resulting in 476 deaths and 677 injuries across fourteen countries.[1]

The danger of Islam goes far beyond its religious definition. It is a socio-political, barbaric movement bent on the worldwide destruction of everything and everyone not bowing at its altars.

In the United States, we have read reports about bombing deaths and injuries in New York City and the detonation

---

1 www.thereligionofpeace.com

of another of several more bombs in New Jersey. Recently, a terrorist was running through a mall in Minnesota, shouting out *Allahu Akbar* as he stabbed nine people before being shot and killed by an off duty policeman.

Government leaders across the nation struggle to avoid calling these solitary attacks by Muslims "Acts of Terror." I wonder what they require to be convinced. It would seem that if it looks like a bomb, explodes like a bomb, and a Muslim has set it off in a crowded area, shouting *Allahu Akbar,* the odds are that it is an act of terrorism.

Many in the United States are having a translation problem with the screaming out of *Allahu Akbar.* They may assume that it is just some sort of prayer proclaiming that God is good.

The truth is that the screaming out of *Allahu Akbar* is meant to strike terror and fear in the hearts of every enemy of Allah, and that includes everyone who is not a jihadist Muslim.

The Islamic translation or meaning is *"Allah is Greater"* or *"Allah is the Greatest."* What is implied is that Allah is greater than you, your god, your religion, your government, your rights, and your life. It is an aggressive declaration of Islamic dominance over all else in the world.

I usually scan through the news each morning and save some of these reports for reference in writing this book. Today, I gave up trying to keep any kind of file dealing with these brutal, heinous acts of violence.

London had just been attacked again and their government issued a *Run, Hide and Tell* order as their preferred method of dealing with the constant aggression from the

INTRODUCTION

growing Muslim population. They did not give an order to Stand and Fight the terrorists, but to run and hide. The Muslim Mayor of London told the people that in a big city like London, you have to expect terrorism.

That probably came as a surprise, I would think, to the people of Tokyo. They have none of this because they have barred Muslims from entering that city and state.

I have read of more mass shootings, murders, rapes, beheadings, and bombs destroying lives and peace than anyone should see in a lifetime. Death and mayhem rule supreme wherever Muslims amass. And they are amassing in hordes across the nations.

I remember awaking a while back to the news that Islamist terrorists had slit the throat [some reports say he was beheaded] of a priest during Mass.

The attack occurred in the northern French town of Saint-Etienne-du-Rouvray, where two men took five people hostage during a morning Mass. One hostage was also seriously wounded. They simply and boldly came to kill a man who served a god who was not Allah.

This came at the heels of the July 14, 2016 massacre by another Islamist radical jihadist in Nice, France who killed eighty-four innocent people and injured another 303.

The terror has gone on at an ever-increasing rate in Europe ever since the tidal waves of young, aggressive Muslims started pouring into Europe at uncontainable numbers.

It is a rare day when we do not hear about more Christians being singled out and tortured, stoned, raped, drowned in cages, maimed, beheaded or burned alive in the Mideast by any one of a number of Islamist terrorist groups. It doesn't even make our nightly news anymore. Recently, there was a story about a British tourist in Dubai who was gang raped and then arrested for having sex with men other than her husband. Their mindset defies all logic.

Another British report stated that Islamic State fighters in Iraq held hundreds of Yazidi women as prisoners and then sold them off as brides for as little as twenty-five dollars. Those refusing were repeatedly raped.

I also read of another brutal mass murder of prisoners in Syria. ISIS posted a graphic video that showed Islamist soldiers executing around 250 Syrian troops. It was too violent to watch.

On November 17, 2016, reports from Iraq detailed the discovery of another mass grave outside of Mosul that contained the remains of about 300 Iraqi policemen, most of whom had been beheaded.

I recently watched a video [only some of it, as it was too brutal] of these butchers taking target practice into a large truck bed filled with teenaged boys, then kicking those still alive into a ditch and machine gunning them down. A terrorist walked among those mortally wounded and shot them in the head. One newsman said it was probably a fake. It puzzles me how they could fake the exploding heads of their victims. It was inhuman.

Another recent video showed a group of ISIS thugs accosting a Muslim woman who was covered from head to feet in a *hijab*, the usual black clothes of the modern, obedient Muslim woman. Apparently their problem was that only her eyes should show, but not her nose and mouth.

INTRODUCTION

They bound her hands behind her and forced her on her knees before a ranting leader of some sort. Men gathered around and shouted and screamed. When the oratory was finished, a man beside the leader put a pistol to the top of her head and casually killed her.

They killed her because they could see a bare nose and mouth, and they left her there, dead in the street. I wonder if her husband or sons were present in the angry mob.

Such is a normal day in the lives of members of the religion of peace.

CRESCENT MOON RISING

The Islamic Invasion of America

CHAPTER ONE

Opening the Gates to the Enemy

Jihadist terrorism has already come to America. Just as it continues to create jihadist havoc, terror, and fear in Europe, it is beginning to flex its strength across our land.

The problem is that the United States of America has been giving up its moral foundation for years, and we have become so *politically correct* and lax in our obedience to common sense that we have a weakened mindset. Our underbelly is soft, and the Islamists see it as an opportunity to move in on the Great Satan and bring it to its knees.

Planeloads of "Muslim refugees" have been flown into America and deposited in places like Boise, Idaho. Mostly single males, they are not there to assimilate, but to bring their lifestyle and customs to America with an expectation for us to assimilate with them.[2]

---

[2] www.wnd.com/2015/04/hundreds-of-muslim-refugees-headed-to-idaho/

We are already seeing brutal rapes and attacks by these hostile immigrants. The American press deftly hides these crimes, but unfortunately, they are simply a normal outcome of Koranic/Hadith theology and sharia sociopolitical norms.

We sit in our comfortable homes in America and sigh about the unfortunate crisis in Europe and the Mideast. But friends, I have news for you. It is already here in America, and is going to get worse. Far worse if we refuse to call it what it is.

USA TODAY, one of the worst cover-up publications, recently reported:

> May 28, 2017. FORT MYERS, Fla.— Two people are dead, including a fourteen-year-old boy and a local high school basketball star, and up to eighteen have been injured after a deadly shooting during teen night at a Florida nightclub. Police said the shooting "is not an act of terror."

I thought: *What do you mean? Not an act of terror?* What determines an act of terror in today's America? The guy doing the violence was a Muslim doing what Muslims do if they are true believers. Let's be clear about the term, *terrorism*.

Wikipedia has a simple definition of terrorism:

> Terrorism is defined in Title 22 Chapter 38 U.S. Code § 2656f as "premeditated, politically motivated violence perpetrated against noncombatant targets by subnational groups or clandestine agents."

OPENING THE GATES TO THE ENEMY

A textbook definition of terrorism includes the following:

> Terrorism is the use of violence or threat of violence especially against civilians in the pursuit of political aims, religious, or ideological change."[3]

Of course this was an act of terror. Americans have been beaten down by any number of acts of terror. Most of it is homegrown terrorism. They call it homegrown violence, but in almost every case, it is done by foreign-born Muslim immigrants or radicalized first generation Muslims. Therefore, the media will not call it Islamic terrorism.

They aren't parachuting in during the middle of the night. They are already here. They are being called to this holy work in the mosques that are now popping up all over America. The references are many. Just Google: *Call to Jihad in American mosques*. There is quite a list.

The Jihadist model is always the same. I will describe the methodology in later chapters. We have become so immune to these Islamic, jihadist horrors being inflicted across the world that some new, horrible atrocity barely catches our eye.

We have been thinking, *"It's tough, but it isn't in my backyard"* for too long. Now it *is* in our backyards, neighborhoods, our businesses and streets. Unchecked, it is gaining momentum and has the capacity to bring the same destruction and hemorrhaging we see across Europe and England.

---

3   en.wikipedia.org/wiki/Definitions_of_terrorism

What can we expect when Muslim leaders and agitators call for American Muslims to act as lone wolf jihadists and attack innocent people in the name of Allah?

This nation has already experienced horrible acts of violence like the December 2, 2015, San Bernardino massacre last year when a radical Muslim and his wife shot up a peaceful office Christmas party, leaving fourteen dead.

Again, on June 13, 2016, in Orlando, Florida, another Muslim radical jihadist massacred forty-nine people and wounded another fifty-three at a gay nightclub. That is just the top of a long list.

You can add the Chattanooga terrorist attack in July of 2105, when a jihadist Muslim staged a suicide attack on a recruiting center at a strip mall and a naval center that left five dead. The service men were unable to protect themselves because our government felt that they should be unarmed.

Have we already forgotten about the Boston Marathon bombing in April of 2015? Those jihadists killed three and wounded and maimed over three hundred more? Again, the terrorists were foreign-born brothers, Jihadist Muslims who felt it their duty to kill Americans.

I will never forget the 2005 Fort Hood massacre by a Muslim psychiatrist who gunned down thirteen of his unarmed fellow servicemen, all the while yelling praises to Allah. What I saw as another act of terrorism, our government leaders at that time refused to label it a Muslim jihadist terror attack and merely called it a case of workplace violence.

We had a similar response from our leaders when Muslim terrorists attacked our embassy in Benghazi, killing our Ambassador and three service men. Not only did U.S. leadership not send support that would have probably saved our citizens, but they also openly lied and told America that it was just a spontaneous response to an anti-Muslim video.

Violence has become commonplace and has numbed this nation into accepting some kind of a *sheep and the wolf* mentality. We have become herds of sheep praying that the wolf will eat some other sheep than ourselves.

We have grown weary with the issues of uncontrolled immigration. It is not just an issue with Muslim immigrants. We are being inundated with alarming numbers of illegal aliens who have been flooding our southern borders.

When that continued without any forceful action, we threw away the immigration keys to America and let our southern states be overwhelmed with illegal aliens by the thousands.

Not only have we turned our backs on a commonsense approach to immigration regulation, we have also exhausted scarce funds by allowing them to stay. We use public money to pay for their healthcare, food, housing, primary education, and even higher education. We then watch as many of them march and demand more.

Even as the angry, young Muslim men poured into Europe and began Islam's takeover by aggressive occupation, we did Europe one better. We began flying them in by the planeload.

When the crimes and acts of terrorism began to escalate, we did another foolish thing. Cities and towns, universities and colleges, began declaring themselves so-called "Safe Havens for any illegal, saint and criminal alike. Across the nation the laws that have protected our people and our sovereignty have been cast aside as trash, all in the name of tolerance or ideological inclusion.

The Governor of California has now declared the entire state to be a Sanctuary State. This law includes protection for murderers, rapists, and pedophiles. The gates are opened wide and you can expect great acts of terrorism are coming to America.

CHAPTER TWO

Has America Lost its Soul?

We have become a *"what difference does it make?"* people. We saturate ourselves with violence as we watch TV, go to the movies, stream content, and play video games. The end result is that we have become desensitized to violence and death. Our passivity towards violence is killing us.

We are actually killing ourselves now at an alarming rate. In 2015, the estimated number of murders in the nation was 15,696. In the first half of 2017, the rate is already at about 9,000.[4]

The number of dead police officers is stacking up. Some are being purposely executed. The massacres in Dallas and Baton Rouge were acts of violence by people encouraged to kill police officers in public demonstrations. But that is just the surface. Just in 2016, 145 policemen were killed in the line of duty, too many of these from intentional violence.[5]

---

4   www.fbi.gov/news/stories/latest-crime-statistics-released
5   www.odmp.org/search/year/2016

Almost every day now, we hear a brief report about another officer shot while on duty. It doesn't even merit a front page article any longer.

What can we expect when angry crowds march down American streets shouting, *"What do we want? Dead Cops! When do we want it? NOW!"*

It isn't just about police officers and Black Lives Matter supporters. We have let wholesale anger and brutal rage take the place of our national civil morality.

Black-on-black killings are increasing at a staggering rate. I read one report that said black-on-black deaths in the U.S. almost outnumber all the U.S. military killed in all our battles in Iraq and Afghanistan.[6] Where are the street marches and protests over this?

Just check out the statistics regarding the murder rate in Chicago. In 2016, there were 762 murders in a city with some of the strictest gun restriction laws in the country. By the end of May, 2017 there were already 255 killings.

While this is primarily a black-on-black situation, we cannot discount the heavy drug gang activities in this same city. It has the third highest city population of Latin Americans in the country and Chicago has been a Mexican cartel drug transport hub for years. The Latino gangs account for a good number of deaths as well.

And Chicago is just one single city among many across the country. Take away the greater population numbers in Chicago and cities like St. Louis, Baltimore, Detroit, New Orleans, and Cleveland have higher per capita murder

---

6   Niall McCarthy, Forbes.com, September 8, 2016

rates. Why aren't marchers and sports figures marching here where these deaths are so much greater than the number killed in confrontation with police, regardless of race and good or bad actions?

But, in today's America, it is easier to disrespect our flag and take an arrogant knee before a football game than to actually face the real issues. Another report said that more black youths have been killed by other black youths than all police shooting deaths this entire century.

This isn't about gun violence or the laws. It is about the wicked hearts of men. It is about a country that has lost its direction.

We probably have 100 million unemployed or underemployed adults in the United States and we have more than forty million more unable or unwilling to work who are on full government assistance. We only have about eighty-five million workers in the private sector, nationwide. We are completely upside down in these unsustainable numbers. We have a non-stop influx of illegal aliens and non-vetted Muslims, and with their need for continuing subsistence, we are heading for a social and economic calamity.

We not only open our borders to the same people group that is committed to destroying Europe, but we now fly them [mostly young single men] into selective small towns and cities across the nation, like Boise, Idaho, without the minimum amount of screening. There are cities like Dearborn, Michigan and Newark, New Jersey, where sharia law is operating openly, and areas in some cities where regular U.S. citizens now fear to enter.

We seem to have lost our national spirit and our very soul. We have accepted unpunished violence as a regular part of life. We have turned the other way when we needed to stand up to it all. What has happened to us?

I read about a group of tourists who waited in line to buy something called "cronuts" in Manhattan, ignoring a dead man lying on a nearby bench in order not to miss a chance at getting their favorite treats. According to police in New York, these shoppers didn't want to get involved. We have forgotten how to care.

What can you expect? We have surrendered morality to self-gratification and political correctness. When did this happen?

CHAPTER THREE

How Did We Become an Anti-Christ Nation?

The beginning of our anti-Christ behavior started in the Garden of Eden, when we became the fallen children of a Holy Heavenly Father. *But that is too simple an answer.*

We saw its beginning in the United States when we took prayer out of the schools. It grew when we allowed the New Age doctrine of self-indulgence to permeate our churches. It festered when we turned the majority of an entire people group into multigenerational welfare families.

It happened when the nation stood by as its fathers began disappearing from their homes, leaving the last several generations of young men and women without fathers to guide their lives in the right directions. It built up when schools became indoctrination camps to the "I'm OK, You're OK" mentality and gave up on expecting accountability.

It happened when many states struck down the laws pertaining to marijuana and whole states like Washington and Colorado lit up the streets and parks in celebration. Never mind that this is an entry-level drug. There is a reason the drug business in the United States runs at about 100 billion dollars a year. We have a whole generation of users who have no anchor.

It grew when we found it easier to deal with abortion than children. Just to give you a little perspective, federally funded abortion mills killed more babies than the population of the entire west coast. Washington State, Oregon, California, Nevada, Idaho, and Utah. The entire populations.[7] The Black Lives Matter activists seem to be unmoved by the killing of over 30 million black babies. It has reached the level of genocide.

Our national agitation and strife have gotten so bad that this angst flows from the kindergartens through the universities and even out onto the sports arenas. Distress, anxiety, anguish, fear, worry, dread, and apprehension are all part of daily life in America. And it is growing at an alarming rate.

Just as recently as the 2016 national elections, we saw the outcome when hundreds of thousands of the new generation called Millennials erupted into the streets because their candidate did not get elected. Their teachers and professors joined them.

Schools and universities all but shut down to care for the weeping students and faculty who lost an election in which most of them did not even vote. We should have been handing out pacifiers to the crowds.

---

[7] saintsalive.com/deadbabiesusa/

Those acts of compliant leadership have all but destroyed the integrity of our entire education system. Universities are now being run by activist students.

It grew when we allowed illegal aliens to pour into our cities and towns. And it mushroomed when our leaders put them on the public dole at a terrible cost to the rest of the legal residents.

We have walked softly around Muslims who have sacrificed their daughters to honor killings because they were seen with a non-Muslim young man from school or work.

Yet our government destroyed a Christian business that does not want to bake a cake for a gay wedding. Christian kids get suspended from school for wearing a Jesus tee shirt yet, we allow Muslin women to cover themselves to the point that they are unidentifiable.

Some of our schools insist on teaching the peaceful religion of Islam to all students, and they are taught to say the *Shahada: "There is no god but Allah; Muhammad is the Messenger of Allah."* Young American women are required to wear Islamic head covers as "student projects." Yet, a Bible or the name of Jesus will prompt immediate discipline.

The heart of America exploded when we legalized sodomy and approved the LGBT movement, and then approved the idea that men's and women's bathrooms were open to anyone who felt like using an opposite sex bathroom that day according to how they identified their gender.

We defied God when we said it was acceptable to feel like a member of the opposite sex and be called by a different name. And if you think that this new federal law that we must allow sexually confused men to use the same bathrooms as our wives and daughters is crazy, just wait for the next step.

Where is the Church?

Where is the church in all of this? In most cases, smiling at the cameras, talking about how good life is in their community (no longer called "church") and rarely mentioning sin. There is rarely a morality checklist for membership in our desire to be "all things to all people."

I don't know about you, but I don't want to go to church to be entertained and leave feeling good about the world and myself. I want to go to a church service and not a gathering. I want to have an encounter with God, not watch a Christian musical performance. I want more of Him, not more of the world and its things. I want a church where people can weep at the altar before a Holy God.

How bad has it become? The American Church, at large, has fallen into apostasy and seeks to please its adherents rather than draw them out of sin and to the foot of the cross. Many new generation churches do not even have a cross.

The Presbyterian Church U.S.A., turned completely away from biblical orthodoxy after lifting up prayers to Allah at its General Assembly meeting in the fall of 2016.

> "Allah bless us and bless our families and bless our
> Lord. Lead us on the straight path – the path of all

prophets: Abraham, Ishmael, Isaac, Moses, Jesus, and Muhammad."

These were the words that rang out over the congregation at The General Assembly of the Presbyterian Church U.S.A. meeting in Portland, Oregon.

Wajidi Said, co-founder of the Muslim Education Trust, led the attendees in the prayer to the Islamic deity – a move arranged by the Ecumenical and Interfaith ministry staff at the assembly. The prayer was part of the "first order of business" during the meeting's opening session, a time dedicated to praying for those affected by the Orlando shooting that occurred just weeks before.

"In the name of Allah, the beneficent, the merciful, let us praise the Lord ... Peace be upon them and peace be upon Allah," Said prayed. He also prayed peace on the "bigots" and "Islamaphobes."

In their defense, I want to mention that at the conclusion of the session, Rev. Gradye Parsons offered an apology to anyone who was offended by the prayer. He assured the congregation that mistakes can be made, but the prayer was not an intentional one. "It was never the intention to offend anyone, and we offer an apology to those who were offended," Rev. Parsons said.

But, back to the spiritual actions based on their apparent lack of knowledge or understanding, the Presbyterian Church still affirms that it will advocate for "positive relationships with people of other religious traditions" and is committed to fighting what they call "the rise in Islamophobia."

Now that I have laid out the groundwork of where we are at in Islamic America today and, yes, vented somewhat, let me take you back to the morning of September 11, 2011, and begin to sort this whole thing out.

CHAPTER FOUR

Remembering September 11, 2001

Like the rest of the country, I was shocked and stunned by the violence and terror of September 11, 2001. Carol and I were at a pastors' retreat and were awakened with a call to turn on our TV.

What we saw was almost surreal; an incomprehensible sight. We wept as we watched. Rushing into our clothes, we hurried and joined the other pastors in the conference room where we went into a time of fervent prayer and intercession.

As the events unfolded, I knew that, as a nation, we would be facing the most serious attack in the history of our country. I also knew it would come through the ranks of a religion, not another nation.

A few years earlier, I read a book called "The Islamic Invasion," by Dr. Robert Morey.[8] Dr. Morey said, "The very DNA of every fervent Muslim, through persuasion

---

8   1992 edition, Harvest House Publishers

and through the sword, is to take the world for Allah. It has been a holy calling from the time of Mohammed's journey to Medina, where he built an army over ten thousand zealots and proclaimed that Allah had instructed them to go forth and cause the nations to bow to Allah and recognize him as Allah's holy prophet or suffer the sword as infidels."

Throughout the centuries, the flames of that fire have burned across the nations, whole cities converting or being slaughtered. That holy war still rages across the world and non-Muslims continue to be slain in vast, incomprehensible numbers.

What was once a Middle-East issue has become global, as Jihadist Muslims have swarmed across the waters and all but consumed Europe and England. Today, it is breaching our own weak and ineffective borders. The Muslims are moving, if not by the millions, at least by the hundreds of thousands into non-Muslim countries at a rate beyond any nation's abilities to control it. Their birth rate alone will make them the majority of any country to which they mass migrate within a century.

Dr. Morey's book was a prophetic wake up call to America. Not only has that battlefield come to America, but it has hit us with a new level and type of violence never seen before on this land. That violence is the core of the Islamic DNA.

It is basic Islamic ideology that the world is divided into two parts. The one is the Islamic "Dar al-Salaam" or House of Islam or House of Peace. Opposing this "Dar al-Salaam" is the "Dar al-Harb" or House of War into which all infidels fall. There can be no peace for Islam until the entire "Dar al-Harb" falls to the "Dar al-Salaam".

So this is a fight to the finish. Islam must be victorious and consume the nations or it must be vanquished. There can be no effective defense against Islam or any effective Christian outreach to its people until we fully understand this volatile religious challenger of our faith and our way of life.

We also need to recognize that the large majority of Muslims living in the United Sates have come here to enjoy lives of peace and prosperity. Many have said that life here is wonderful. They contribute much to our society. Many fathers and husbands are able to release their daughters and wives to live life freely, openly, without degradation or sexual mutilation in the name of Allah. Many can go to school, be educated, have careers, drive cars, go to the movies, and marry whom they love.

However, it has been clearly evidenced by their public silence that even the most placid of Muslims in America are accustomed to even the worst of the raging by screaming Jihadists. They know what the core of their faith is and many live in actual fear of those Muslims who would judge them for any negative reaction.

After speaking to many who study these things, I would guess that over 90% of the Muslims in America live such lives in peace, having Americanized their faith without compromising their beliefs. *I actually believe the figure is closer to 80%, but will be cautiously conservative and use just the 90% here.*

In not compromising their beliefs they have brought a quiet base of Muslim "occupation" to this country. That allows the radicals to come to an established "beach head." While this majority would never consider an act of terrorism, it is a rare moment when we hear this group decrying the violent acts of their brethren.

CHAPTER FIVE

If Just a Tenth of a Tenth of a Tenth

In spite of the statistic that 90% of Muslims live in the United States in peace, that leaves 10% who maintain the fundamentalism of radical, Jihadist Islam. The percentage is small, but the actual number of such fundamental Muslims in America alone is now probably over 750,000. These are the people who say nothing when a fellow Muslim father kills his daughter because she fell in love with an American boy.

If we took just 10% of that number, we would have seventy-five thousand Muslims here who maintain that America is the great Satan the Islamic extremists shout about. That adds up to about fifteen hundred Muslim Jihadists per state. In the minds of those radicals, we must either bow to Allah or be slain in his holy name.

A tenth of even that small minority of radicals leaves us with a pool of about 7,500 violent extremists. These are Jihadist Muslims with a grave potential for terrorist behavior. I would estimate that 40% to 50% of the young men ferried in from Syria can be added to that number. They are ready to act as "lone wolf" Jihadists and murderers.

It is interesting that while Europe and America bring them in by the boatloads, not a single Arab nation will take in these Muslim "refugees"—many of whom are Jihadist activists.

These super-radicals are such as those who attacked us on September 11, 2001, living here among us, as an Islamic Fifth Column. Among that number are Muslims like the couple that murdered fourteen of the husband's fellow workers in San Bernardino, California, in December 2015.

For those too young to remember the Second World War, that Fifth Column was a group of people, although residing, even as citizens of the United States, acted traitorously and subversively on behalf of an enemy.

On a global basis, there are over 1.6 billion Muslims. We are told that 20%, or about 300 million, fall into this larger fundamentalist group, and over thirty million Muslims of that group have a violent, Jihad worldview.

Following just my one tenth of 1% formula, we are still left with a global pool of over three million fanatic zealots out there who can easily become "terrorists for Allah."

The word *Jihad is* used quite often. It represents a holy war or crusade.

1. A holy war waged on behalf of Islam as a religious duty.

2. A crusade for a principle or belief.[9]

---

[9] Merriam Webster Collegiate Dictionary.

IF JUST A TENTH OF A TENTH OF A TENTH

My estimates in this area were confirmed when I watched an MSNBC special report during which an Islamic expert calculated that she (Dr. Hunter) estimated the number of extreme radicals in countries where Islam is in the majority, to be double my figures.

This is going to be a long and difficult war against the likes of the late Osama bin Laden and his ever-emerging imitators. We must know what we are dealing with before it is too late.

However, through all this, we must never let fear and anger against that one tenth of 1% jade our hearts and actions against those who live among us as friends and neighbors.

We must let them see the love of Christ in us, remembering that we are all made in His image, and that His Son died for us all. Anything less would be to deny the call of Christ in our lives.

President Bush commented at the destruction of the Twin Towers that while we need to be in a state of high alert, we should not fall into a state of fear or revenge. As Christians, we especially need to be in intercession for this people group and prepare ourselves to be His hand extended.

We must be His ambassadors, girded up and prepared according to the sixth chapter of the book of Ephesians, with our feet shod with the preparation of the gospel of peace so we may open our mouths to boldly to make known the mystery of the gospel.

However, as we will discuss later in this book, during the administration of Barack Obama, approximately a million Muslims have poured into the United States. Extending our hand to them is very difficult, because for the most part they shun any kind of integration into the American way of life.

CHAPTER SIX

Accidentally Stirring the Wrath of Islam

Some years ago, I was speaking at Utah State University in Logan, Utah on the subject: "Mormonism – the American Islam." I drew a comparison between the amazingly similar claims of Mohammed and Joseph Smith.

Both men claimed visitations of an angel of light, both claimed to be God's last and greatest prophet, and they each claimed that they were called to bring forth God's final, pure word for mankind: the Koran and the Book of Mormon. Neither was shy in his affirmation of his holy calling.

In fact, in 1838, during the Missouri Mormon troubles, the Mormon Prophet actually declared,

> "I will be a second Mohammed to this generation… whose motto, in treating for peace, was 'the Alcoran [Koran] or the Sword,' so shall it be eventually with us, 'Joseph Smith or the Sword.'"

In my presentation, I compared their similar doctrines of the nature of God, personal salvation, and the after life with those of orthodox Christianity.

The auditorium soon became too small for the large gathering and we filled the large commons area of the Student Union beyond capacity. We finally overflowed throughout the large student center and entrance.

USU had certainly grown from that small Agricultural College I attended in the early 1950s. The meeting was packed with Muslims and Islamic clerics, all of whom were extremely offended at any reference to Allah, the Koran, and visibly agitated and angry that I would draw as offensive a comparison with any similarity to Mormonism.

During the presentation of my evidence, there was much murmuring and shouting. When I opened the floor for the "Question and Answer" time, I faced a number of very agitated and verbally abusive Muslims.

In fact, the Muslim interaction completely overshadowed any dialogue on Mormonism. Were there not security guards all around, I am sure there would have been serious difficulties. The next day, I met with two local Muslim leaders and began a series of dialogues that forced me to take a deep look at Islam's history, tenets of belief, extreme volatility, and its comparisons to orthodox Christianity.

An extremely militant proselytizing program was already under way in Logan, Utah and in most major cities and in every State University we visited. Campus Muslim groups are fomenting discord on almost every American campus.

ACCIDENTALLY STIRRING THE WRATH OF ISLAM

The Muslims have made the Mormon missionary effort look pale in comparison. As orthodox Christians, we are going to have to deal with what has become the most aggressive assault on Christianity in its history.

It has taken deep root in our schools, universities, and public offices. Local grocery stores now regularly sell Halal meats and poultry that are prepared with minimal FDA oversight, so as not to offend the Muslims.

CHAPTER SEVEN

The Faith of Mohammed

Let's look at the faith of Mohammed. When he was born in Mecca in 570 A.D., the black *Kaaba* was the religious center of all Arabia.

In Mohammed's day, approximately 360 idols, or allahs, were worshipped there, with each idol's tribe of worshipers coming to the great courtyard to bow before their own deity.

One of those deities or allahs was the god of the Quarish tribe, of which Mohammed was a member. When the Quarish tribe took control of Mecca, all the idols except Allah, the idol of their tribe, were destroyed.

The Koran tells us that Mohammed drove the other idols away; his god was now the only god and he was its messenger. But he kept the Kaaba as a holy, sacred place. He obligated every believer to make a pilgrimage to the stone at least once in his lifetime (Sura 22:26-37).

The central prayer or declaration of Islam, to this day, is the The Shahada: *"There is no God but (this) Allah and Mohammed is his prophet."*

We most often hear the Muslim cry of "Allahu Akbar" which means: *Allah [their deity] is Great.* Unfortunately, we hear it too often during acts of Islamic Terrorism.

Many people believe that Islam, Judaism, and Christianity are all just kissing cousins. In fact, many Christian pastors erroneously teach that Allah is just another name for the biblical God whom we worship.

Hopefully, this comes from ignorance rather than ecumenical foolishness.

In this study, we are going to examine Islam from the orthodox Christian perspective; what it is that Muslims teach and believe, and how it differs from Christianity. We are also going to look at why the last few years have brought Islamic terrorism across the world.

We will look at the well-planned mass migration of primarily militant Muslims that is destroying Europe and is now moving into America.

Finally, I will share how to reach the Muslims with the true gospel of peace and the cross of Christ. Let's equip you to share the claims of Jesus Christ in a loving and compassionate way with the Muslim.

CHAPTER EIGHT
A Word to the Muslim Reader

I know that Muslims, as well as Christians, are reading this book. I would like to pause and address our Muslim readers for just a moment:

Muslim readers, you need to know that I appreciate you taking the time to see how your faith is seen from the Christian viewpoint. There will be some things that you read that will cause you to be in strong disagreement. I apologize for offending you, but I will speak out on the issue. I know of no other way in which we can dialogue honestly.

Hopefully, we can discuss these issues in truth and in love for one another. As the Book of Proverbs says:

> As iron sharpens iron, So a man sharpens the countenance of his friend.
> Proverbs 27:17 NKJV

We need to stand on words of truth that will bring us all to the God of truth and life's perspective in this matter.

"All the paths of the LORD are mercy and truth, to such as keep His covenant and His testimonies" (Psalm 25:10 NKJV).

> *Oh, send out Your light and Your truth!*
> *Let them lead me...*
>
> Psalm 43:3 NKJV

> *Sanctify them by Your truth. Your word is truth.*
>
> John 17:17 NKJV

And from Islamic scripture:

> And mix not truth with falsehood, nor conceal the truth *[i.e. Muhammad Peace be upon him is Allah's Messenger and his qualities are written in your Scriptures, the Taur (Torah), and the Injeel (Gospel)]* while you know (the truth).
>
> Sura 2:42

Please understand that in the United States, where freedom of religion and freedom of speech are still constitutional guarantees, we have the freedom to discuss, to consider, and to think and speak out concerning religious issues.

Sometimes what is said will offend you, but that is the core value in the American guarantee of free speech. You are certainly free to respond with reason and peace.

We are not in countries such as Saudi Arabia or Iran, where we would have religious police at our doors, confiscating such studies as this, arresting us, even beheading us, because in such nations there simply is no freedom of religion.

That is not freedom of thought and action. You cannot question Mohammed or the Koran in such a controlled state.

But we are not in a Muslim nation. We are in a free nation where our constitution gives us the freedom and right to think and act for ourselves.

In things of faith, this is so vitally important, and as such, it is a major difference between our cultures and faiths. The value of dialogue brings greater appreciation and meaning to things of faith. If you are living here in America, you already understand these principles.

CHAPTER NINE
Islam Across the World

Islam is a rapidly growing religion, both spiritually and geographically. Today, Islam makes up almost one quarter of the world's population.

Islam has a total of about 1.62 billion members, or 23% of the entire world's population. About forty-nine countries have a Muslim majority. Over 60% of the world's Muslims live in South and Southeast Asia.

Islam itself consists of two major divisions – the mainstream Sunni at about 87-90% (the largest), and the more radical Shi'ites. The mystical tradition of Sufism includes many Sunnis and some Shi'ites. Ten to 13% are Shia Muslims.

Surprisingly, when most people think about Muslims, they immediately think of the Middle East or North Africa, but in fact, only 20% of the world's Muslims live in the Middle East or North Africa. Most of them live in other countries. While these figures are now more than a few years old, they will give you a general idea of the magnitude and complexity of the Muslim world.

The Arab world all together – including all of the Middle East and North Africa – has less than 200 million Muslims. The largest Muslim country is Indonesia, with over 182 million Muslims, 80% of its population.

Bangladesh has 115 million, 88% of its population. India has 108 million Muslims, approximately 11% of its population.

Pakistan, where riots and anti-American demonstrations often rage, has 136 million Muslims, 95% of its people. Even if only 1% of that population is made up of rabid fundamentalist radicals, it totals 1.36 million people who stood with Osama bin Laden and now stand with the terrible reign of terror being wrought by ISIS.

To the surprise of many people, there is a large Muslim population in China. In fact, nearly thirty million Muslims live in China. The former Soviet Union, the whole Southern tier, along the border with Afghanistan, Iran, Syria, and Iraq, and all across to Turkey, is home for more than forty-one million Muslims.

In Turkey, there are about sixty-two million, 92% of the population, and in Iran, sixty-three million Muslims make up 97% of its population – and on it goes.

Islam is now the second largest religion in Europe. In Great Britain, there are now over one-and-a-half million Muslims, with some fifteen hundred Mosques.

With the recent influx of hundreds of thousands of Muslims into European nations, it is their goal to continue to flow into these nations by great numbers and explode the Muslim birth rates in order to gain majority numbers.

In Germany alone, the Muslim Crisis has changed the face of Germany forever. In a recent report, the following comments were made:

> Critics of Germany's open-door immigration policy are warning that the recent surge in Germany's Muslim population – which *surpassed* six million in 2016 for the first time – has already changed the face of the country forever.
>
> Mass migration is fast-tracking the rise of Islam in Germany, as evidenced by the proliferation of *no-go zones*, *sharia courts*, *polygamy*, *child marriages*, and *honor violence*. Mass migration has also been responsible for social chaos, including *jihadist attacks*, a *migrant rape epidemic*, a *public health crisis*, *rising crime*, and a rush by German citizens to *purchase weapons* for self-defense – and even to *abandon* Germany altogether.
>
> The government has not said how it plans to integrate potentially millions of additional Muslims into German society. The price for reversing Germany's demographic decline appears to be the further Islamization of Germany under the guise of multiculturalism.[10]

In the United States, Islam was virtually nonexistent thirty years ago. But, because of heavy immigration from Muslim countries and mass uncontrolled migration of

---

10 www.gatestoneinstitute.org/9892/germany-muslims-demographic

hundreds of thousands of Muslims, there is now an Islamic population of over seven million.

Many Muslims have fled the oppression of the Islamic states, seeking freedom in the United States. Many others now come to America to bring radical Islam to our shores. The most frustrating part of this is that our own government brings them in by the planeload and puts them on the American Dream-Gravy Train immediately.

I read a recent news article about a Muslim man who was settled in a small town in Idaho. He was receiving public financial assistance for the three wives in his home and over a dozen children. His monthly take looked to be over ten thousand dollars a month. Nice non-work if you can get it.

Muslim-based sects such as the Nation of Islam (which appeals especially to African-Americans) and Bahai (which proclaims the unity of the human race) have special appeal to many Americans.

In a 2016 sermon, Nation of Islam leader Louis Farrakhan, now eighty-two, said in Miami at Mt. Zion Missionary Baptist Church that the time has come for ten thousand black volunteers to rise up and kill white Americans.

He added, *"Retaliation is a prescription from God to calm the breasts of those whose children have been slain. So if the federal government will not intercede in our affairs, then we must rise up and kill those who kill us. Stalk them and kill them and let them feel the pain of death that we are feeling."*

CHAPTER TEN

A People Cut Off from the Christian World View

The Lord gave Christians a great commission – to go into the entire world and proclaim the good news of Jesus Christ. But we have not carried that great commission, as we should, into the Muslim world. Only about 2% of American missionaries have been involved in Muslim ministries.

We have one or two Christian missionaries for every one million Muslims. Islam now represents the single greatest challenge to Christianity.

No matter how peaceful many Muslims may seem on the surface, their core doctrine allows for no other faith to legitimately exist within the borders of its control and influence. That makes it extremely difficult to openly bring the Gospel to them.

Recently, we read about large numbers of Muslims converting to Christianity in Europe. Reliable data is almost impossible to provide, but anecdotal evidence indicates that many see the freedom and lack of fear and violence in their Christian neighbors and are drawn away from the brutality of their religion and make the change. Peace doesn't often come with conversion, however. Many are beaten or killed as they head home from a Christian church by their Muslim neighbors.

We continue to be bombarded with media reports of how the Muslims in America are beset with fear because we misinterpret their faith as one with roots of aggression against Jews and Christians. The media has been waging an information battle against this ideology, proclaiming that Islam is a religion of peace and love. Former President Obama proclaimed this publicly at every opportunity.

That this is not evident in any of the Islamic countries is beside the point. The continual path of murder and death from the Palestinian Hamas' suicide and knifing squads proves just the opposite. The pictures of Palestinians rejoicing in the streets, as they celebrated the Muslim extremist mass murders of 9/11, confirmed the true heart of the mid-east Muslim.

Hal Lindsey reported at the time that one Muslim cleric, praying for peace at the National Cathedral, alongside our President and many mighty men of God on that Friday Day Of Remembrance, wasn't that patriotic. That same Islamic leader was at a rally in California a few months earlier where an American flag, along with an Israeli flag, was burned.

We must be cautious. While the Islamic leaders of the Middle East were smiling softly at the cameras for CNN and their American audience, they had this to say to their own people, as reported by the Muslim *Palestinian Times*:

Palestinian Scholars Forbade all Muslims from Joining American Campaign Against Afghanistan.

Muslim Ulema (religious scholars) throughout Palestine issued an edict that prohibited Muslim States from joining the American-led crusade against Afghanistan or any other Muslim countries.

A Fatwah, or religious ruling, issued recently by the League of Palestinian Ulema, which represents over five hundred religious scholars and academics in Palestine, stated that:

> "...it is amply clear in light of the Holy Qur'an and the traditions of our Holy Prophet (peace be upon him) that it is inadmissible for Muslims to enter into alliance with non-Muslims against fellow Muslims."

The edict cited evidence from the Qur'an and Sunnah (the sayings, actions, and silences of the Prophet) to that effect. It warned Muslims against falling into the trap of fighting and killing fellow Muslims under the rubric of "fighting terrorism."

Several similar Fatwahs were issued throughout the Muslim world, all forbidding Muslims from joining the American campaign against the Taliban in Afghanistan.

Sheikh Ibrahim Zaid al-Kilani, a prominent Islamic figure in Jordan, also issued a strongly-worded statement admonishing Arab regimes against "joining ranks with the disbelievers against fellow Muslims." He invoked the Qur'anic verse that states, "Whoever joins them (the disbelievers) is one of them."[11]

---

11 *Palestinian Times*, Web Report, October 2001.

CHAPTER ELEVEN

A Seventh Century People in a Twenty-First Century World

To understand Islam, perhaps the key factor is to realize that Islam must be understood in the religious and cultural context of seventh century Arabia.

What Mohammed did was to raise seventh century tribal culture to the status of both divine and state law. In fact, Islam is the deification of seventh century Arabian culture. Unless you understand the historical context of when and where Mohammed was born, you will never understand Islam.

Dr. Arthur Arberry, the head of Mid-Eastern Studies at Cambridge University and one of the great Arabic scholars said:

> "Islam is a peculiarly Arabian religion because Islam is a religion and culture, and as a religion and culture, they are one. It must be understood," he said,

"in terms of its essential identification with Seventh Century culture."

Islam imposes its seventh century Arabian culture, in its political expression, in its family affairs, in its dietary laws, in its clothing, in its religious rites, in its educational systems, and in its language. They are religiously and socially compelled to impose seventh century Arab culture on the rest of the cultures in the world.

Mohammed took the political laws that governed seventh century Arabian tribes, and literally made them the laws of Allah, their God. In such tribes, the sheik or chief of the nomadic tribes had absolute authority. There was no concept of civil or personal rights in seventh century Arabia.

This is why Islamic countries are inevitably ruled by dictators or strong men who rule as despots. The very concept of democratic rule and a freely-elected government is an alien concept.

There are twenty-two Arab nations today, and not one of them is a modern democracy. The list includes Algeria, Bahrain, the Comoros Islands, Djibouti, Egypt, Iraq, Jordan, Kuwait, Lebanon, Libya, Morocco, Mauritania, Oman, Palestine, Qatar, Saudi Arabia, Somalia, Sudan, Syria, Tunisia, the United Arab Emirates, and Yemen.

The more that Islamic Fundamentalism gains dominance, the more a nation is plunged back into the dark ages of seventh century Arabia. The despots today of Libya, Iran, Iraq, Syria, Afghanistan, the Sudan, and Yemen are merely examples of such Arabian tyranny grafted into modern times.

Because there was no concept of personal freedom or civil rights in tribal life of seventh century Arabia, Islamic law today does not recognize freedom of speech, freedom of religion, freedom of assembly, or freedom of the press. In such a society, women have no rights, except those granted by a father or a husband.

The denial of freedom of religion is why non-Muslims, such as Christians, are routinely denied the most basic of human rights, often physically attacked or jailed. These incidents are usually violent. The many videos of ISIS beheading groups of Christians or burning them alive are grim testimonies of their violent hearts.

This conflict is one major reason that modern-thinking Arabs have immigrated to the United States in such numbers. It often comes at a great cost, including family alienation. We need to understand and have compassion for them.

Yet, even these who have fled such a life remain silent as the Islamic terrorist attacks continue to grow across the nations and now have become regular events even in the United States. This violence against non-believers of Islam is in the deepest core of their faith.

CHAPTER TWELVE

The Women of Islam

One of the most demeaning practices of Islam is its barbaric treatment of women. Women are considered property in most sects of Islam. They are not allowed to have ownership of any kind of property.

Approximately 75% of Muslim women suffer female circumcision in a most barbaric, painful ritual designed to make them obedient and docile. Just recently, a Muslim female doctor in Michigan was charged with mutilating young Muslim girls which were patients of hers. Another doctor, Dr. Qanta Ahmed, wrote this:

> A woman physician, Dr. Jumana Nagarwala, was charged in federal court for performing female genital mutilation on two girls as young as seven in a medical clinic in Livonia, Michigan, outside Detroit.
>
> Authorities suspect the Henry Ford Hospital emergency physician had been secretly performing

these brutal procedures since 2005, impacting many more children. Henry Ford Hospital has placed the physician on administrative leave while she is on bail. (She is alleged to have performed these procedures at a clinic, not at a Ford facility.)

As a physician in whom my patients place their trust, I am sickened. More importantly, I am enraged, and you should be too.

The United States designates female genital mutilation a federal crime (the literal butchering of a woman or girl's female genitalia) for good reason. Tragically Michigan is one of *twenty-six states that have failed to enact laws against the practice.*

Around the world, *more than 200 million* infants and girls are mutilated by female genital mutilation/cutting (FGM/C). Most are cut between infancy and age fifteen, but women up to age forty-nine have been thus mutilated.[12]

Orthodox Muslim women are dressed from head to toes in clothes that cover all but the eyes, and often a veil covers these. Their illiteracy rate is higher than 75%.

It is interesting that what an illiterate nomadic tribeswoman wore in the desert in seventh century Arabia is still mandated as the dress code for Muslim women today. It's a denial of civil rights to women and is reflective of the Islamic Arabian culture and its low view of women.

---

[12] www.thedailybeast.com/and-now-female-genital-mutilation-comes-to-america

Within the mosques, men are often advised on the proper manner of wife beatings and what behaviors justify increased intensity of the beatings. Love and forgiveness and mercy are not part of the package.

Today, Muslim men still have the right to have up to four wives, and while polygamy has been a crime in the United States for over a century, many Muslims here quietly practice it without a word from the authorities.

Families regularly barter young, under-aged Muslim girls away into marriage to older Muslim men. The Islamic faith condones pedophilia. Therefore, contemporary pedophilic Islamic marriages are a very common Muslim practice around the globe.

> And (as for) those of your women who have despaired of menstruation, if you have a doubt, their prescribed time shall be three months, and of those too who have not had their courses; and (as for) the pregnant women, their prescribed time is that they lay down their burden; and whoever is careful of (his duty to) Allah He will make easy for him his affair.
>
> Quran Sura 65:4

Our mothers and before them our grandmothers married when they were barely twelve. Good upbringing makes a girl ready to perform all marital duties at that age.[13]

---

13 Grand Mufti of Saudi Arabia, Sheikh Abdul Aziz Al-Sheikh

A nine-year-old girl has the same sexual capacities like a woman of twenty and over.[14]

A man can marry a girl younger than nine years of age, even if the girl is still a baby being breastfed. A man, however, is prohibited from having intercourse with a girl younger than nine; other sexual acts such as foreplay, rubbing, kissing, and sodomy is allowed.

A man having intercourse with a girl younger than nine years of age has not committed a crime, but only an infraction, if the girl is not permanently damaged. If the girl, however, is permanently damaged, the man must provide for her all her life.

But this girl will not count as one of the man's four permanent wives. He also is not permitted to marry the girl's sister.[15]

The Hijab

"O Prophet! Tell your wives and your daughters and the women of the believers to draw their cloaks (veils) all over their bodies. That will be better, that they should be known (as free respectable women) so as not to be annoyed."

Quran 33:59

---

14 Sheikh Mohamed Ibn Abderrahmane Al-Maghraoui
15 The late Ayatollah Khomeini of Iran, Supreme Leader of the Islamic Revolution

"Say to the believing women that they should lower their gaze and protect their private parts (from sins); and they should not display their beauty and ornaments except what appear thereof…"

Quran 24:31

When a girl reaches the menstrual age, it is not proper that anything should remain exposed except this and this. He pointed to the face and hands.

Abu Dawud

The purpose of hijab is to cover the awrah, and awrah varies in different situations and amongst different groups of people. In most cases, it refers to the intimate parts of the female body. Pretty much from the neck to the knees and beyond. I picked up some information from a few Muslim websites to be sure I described it correctly.

They began with the conditions of hijab for a woman in public and amongst non-mahram men. As long as these conditions are fulfilled, a woman may wear whatever she pleases, except when a husband, father, or male family member disagrees.

1. The hijab (covering) must conceal the entire body except the face and the hands.

2. It should not be translucent or tight. Tight clothes, even if they conceal the color of the skin, still describe the size and shape of the body or part of it, and create vivid images.

3. It should not attract the attention of the opposite gender; thus it should not be extravagant or excessively opulent. Nor should jewelry and makeup be on display.

4. It should not be a garment worn because of vanity or to gain popularity or fame. The females usually wear black and other dark colors, but other colors are permissible; a woman must not, however, wear colorful clothes because of vanity.

5. It should not be perfumed. This prohibition applies to both the body and the clothes.

6. It should not resemble the clothing worn by men.

7. It should not resemble the clothing that is specific to the non-Muslims.

Women's Rights

While most democratic nations have openly accepted the people of the Islamic faith within our countries and have encouraged them to worship freely, as they desire, the same is not true in their own countries.

You might remember back to an incident that took place back during the Gulf War. On March 10, 1991, the

New York Times magazine reported the following story about women's rights in Saudi Arabia, our key partner in the Muslim world today.

The crisis in the Gulf War had spawned a messy and much-publicized demonstration by women who dumped their chauffeurs and drove in a convoy, defying a ban on women driving in Saudi Arabia. The incident prompted a vicious campaign against them by religious fanatics with government acquiescence.

Underlying these strains was the question of how much power the religious establishment should have, in particular, the religious police who patrol the streets and shopping malls, telling the women to cover their faces, and beating those who defied them.

It certainly had nothing to do with democratic process and living standards. The only people with spine in their society were the forty-seven women bravely who drove their cars, one Saudi intellectual has said.

And look what happened to them – they were thrown to the wolves. The government punished them as severely as it would any criminal. Virtually all those who taught (school) were dismissed by order of the king. The women, as well as their husbands, were forbidden to leave the kingdom.

They were forbidden to speak with foreign reporters or to discuss their situations with any outsider. They were warned of further reprisals if they attempted to drive again and stage another demonstration. We are talking about the simple act of driving a car.

It makes you wonder what we were trying to defend over in Saudi Arabia. But the Saudi government's treatment of these women was mild compared to their treatment by the Islamic religious establishment. They were reviled by the fundamentalist sheiks who denounced them from one of the kingdom's most powerful political platforms, the Mosque Opus.

In the Friday services after the demonstration the women were branded as "Red communists, dirty American secularists, whores and prostitutes, fallen women and advocators of vice."

Their names, occupations, addresses, and phone numbers were distributed in leaflets at the mosques and other public places. One leaflet accused them of having denounced Islam, an offense punishable by death in Saudi Arabia.

And these women were all educated. Some of them had PhDs, with most of them teaching at the University there. Some were medical doctors. They were threatened with beatings, death by stoning, or beheading.

What had they done? They had stepped into cars and drove them. Several of the women that drove the cars remained unrepentant; hoping that eventually the issue of their status would be addressed.

"The issue is not driving," one of them said. "It is that here in Saudi Arabia; I function as a person only from the belly button to the knees."

Has anything changed in Islam during the years since that single demonstration? Not such that you could tell. American Muslims, whose wives do drive cars, remained silent. I would hope it was out of fear of reprisal rather than agreement. At least they would have an excuse, as cowardly is it would be.

The Muslim nations all stand by silently as Christians and Jews are openly attacked and slaughtered across the Islamic world, and our own heads of state sit with fawning smiles for photo ops with the same men who turn their eyes from the wanton butcheries all around them.

A Former Muslim Woman writes:
The Joys of Being a Muslim Woman
by Nonie Darwish, a woman born in Egypt as a Muslim

In the Muslim faith a Muslim man can marry a child as young as one year old and have sexual intimacy with this child, consummating the marriage by nine.

The dowry is given to the family in exchange for the woman (who becomes his slave) and for the purchase of the private parts of the woman, to use her as a toy.

Even though a woman is abused, she can not obtain a divorce. To prove rape, the woman must have (four) male witnesses.

Often after a woman has been raped, she is returned to her family and the family must return the dowry. The family has the right to execute her (an honor killing) to restore the honor of the family.

Husbands can beat their wives "at will" and the man does not have to say why he has beaten her. The husband is permitted to have four wives and a temporary wife for an hour (prostitute) at his discretion.

The *sharia* Muslim law controls the private as well as the public life of the woman.

In the Western World (UK), Muslim men are starting to demand sharia law so the wife cannot obtain a divorce and he can have full and complete control of her. It is amazing and alarming how many of our sisters and daughters attending American Universities are now marrying Muslim men and submitting themselves and their children unsuspectingly to the sharia law.

By passing this on, enlightened women may avoid becoming a slave under sharia law.

Ripping the West in Two

Author and lecturer Nonie Darwish says the goal of radical Islamists is to impose sharia law on the world, ripping Western law and liberty in two. She recently authored the book, *Cruel and Usual Punishment: The Terrifying Global Implications of Islamic Law.*

Darwish was born in Cairo and spent her childhood in Egypt and Gaza before immigrating to America in 1978, when she was eight years old. Her father died while leading covert attacks on Israel. He was a high-ranking Egyptian military officer stationed with his family in Gaza.

When he died, he was considered a "shahid," a martyr for jihad. His posthumous status earned Nonie and her family an elevated position in Muslim society.

But Darwish developed a skeptical eye at an early age. She questioned her own Muslim culture and upbringing. She converted to Christianity after hearing a Christian preacher on television.

In her latest book, Darwish warns about creeping sharia law – what it is, what it means, and how it is manifested in Islamic countries.

For the West, she says radical Islamists are working to impose sharia on the world. If that happens, Western civilization will be destroyed. Westerners generally assume all religions encourage a respect for the dignity of each individual.

Islamic law (sharia) teaches that non-Muslims should be subjugated or killed in this world. Peace and prosperity for one's children is not as important as assuring that Islamic law rules everywhere in the Middle East and eventually in the world.

While Westerners tend to think that all religions encourage some form of the golden rule, sharia teaches two systems of ethics – one for Muslims and another for non-Muslims. Building on tribal practices of the seventh century, sharia encourages the side of humanity that wants to take from and subjugate others.

While Westerners tend to think in terms of religious people developing a personal understanding of and relationship with God, sharia advocates executing people who ask difficult questions that could be interpreted as criticism.

It's hard to imagine, that in this day and age, Islamic scholars agree that those who criticize Islam or choose to stop being Muslim should be executed.

Sadly, while talk of an Islamic reformation is common and even assumed by many in the West, such murmurings in the Middle East are silenced through intimidation.

While Westerners are accustomed to an increase in religious tolerance over time, Darwish explains how petro dollars are being used to grow an extremely intolerant form of political Islam in her native Egypt and elsewhere.

In twenty years there will be enough Muslim voters in the UK to elect the Prime Minister by themselves! Rest assured they will do so... You can look at how they have taken over several towns in the U.S.A. Dearborn, Michigan, is one... and there are others.

I think everyone in the UK should be required to read this, but with the ACLU, there is no way this will be widely publicized unless each of us sends it on![16]

It is too bad that so many are disillusioned with life and Christianity to accept Muslims as peaceful. Some may be, but they have an army that is willing to shed blood in the name of Islam. The peaceful support the warriors with their finances and own kind of patriotism to their religion.

While America is getting rid of Christianity from all public sites and erasing God from the lives of children, the Muslims are planning a great jihad on America.

---

16 Darwish, Nonie, *Wholly Different: Why I Chose Biblical Values Over Islamic Values*, Washington, D.C.: Regnery Faith, 2017.

CHAPTER THIRTEEN

The Gods of the Seventh Century

The culture of Mohammed's world was very animistic. Every Arab tribe had its sacred, magic stone(s) that they believed protected the tribe, sitting resident in the Kaaba. Mohammed's particular tribe had adopted a black stone and had set it in the Kaaba.

This magical black stone was kissed when people came on their pilgrimages and worshipped at the Kaaba. It was probably an asteroid or a meteorite, a moonstone, which they viewed as being divine. All the nomadic tribes had their own tribal deities.

The dominant religion just prior to Mohammed was Sabianism, a religion in which heavenly bodies were worshipped. The moon was viewed as a male deity, and they used a lunar calendar. Their pagan rite of fasting began with the appearance of the crescent moon.

Fasting was later adopted as one of the five pillars of faith of Islam. Fasting, based on the lunar calendar, in the ninth month of Ramadan, already pre-existed in the Arab culture before Mohammed was even born.

The term "Allah" is a purely Arabic term used in reference to any Arabian deity. Muslims claim that Allah is the same God as worshipped by Christians, just under another name. Yet, if you look at the history of it, it is very different.

The tribe into which Mohammed was born was particularly devoted to their Allah, which was the moon god. It was represented by a black stone or meteorite, which they believed had come down from heaven.

In Arabia, the sun god was viewed as female, and the moon was perceived as the male god. In pre-Islamic times, Allah, the moon god, was married to the sun god, and together they produced three goddesses called The Daughters of Allah.

They were viewed as being at the top of the pantheon of Arabian deities, those three hundred and sixty idols in the Kaaba at Mecca.

Do not ever accept Allah as just another name of the true and living God, the God of Abraham, Isaac, and Jacob. This Arabian stone deity was also the god of the Ishmaelites. Ishmael was not the son of the covenant. Isaac was the son of the covenant.

The symbol of the worship of the moon god, Allah, in pre-Islamic Arab culture throughout the Middle East, was the crescent moon. Today, the crescent moon is on every flag of an Islamic nation. A crescent moon, the symbol of Allah, the moon god, sits on top of every mosque.

Mohammed, the prophet of Islam, was born in 570 A.D. and lived for sixty-two years, dying in 632. At the time he was born, Mecca was the center of trade and religious activity. Mohammed was a camel driver until the age of twenty-five when he met and married a lady who was fifteen years his senior. She was forty years old, a wealthy lady.

For the next fifteen years, he ran her family fruit business in Mecca. It wasn't until he was forty years old that he began to receive his revelations. He would go, as seekers of truth would, up to a cave that was about three miles northeast of Mecca to pray and meditate.

According to Muslim tradition, the angel Gabriel came to Mohammed in a mountain cave called Hira. Actually there are four different statements of what happened (in the Koran) which contradict each other.

The Muslims say that it was Gabriel, and they took this as a sign that Mohammed was the true prophet to the Arabs. After meditating there off and on for two years, Muslims say that Mohammed received revelations, during which he would go into epileptic fits.

That's what Muslims believe they were. He would shake, he would perspire, and he would foam at the mouth. Whether they were epileptic or even demonic, he claimed that during these fits, he received revelations from an angel of light, which he claimed was Gabriel.

What were the revelations? They were written down into what is known as the Koran, the Islamic scripture, or holy book. They were not written down until years later because Mohammed was uneducated and probably did not know how to read or write.

The main message that Mohammed communicated was that there was no god but Allah, that he was the one true god who created everything.

The second thing he taught was that man is God's slave, and it is his first duty to submit to God and to obey him. The term Islam, in Arabic, means submission, and a Muslim is one who submits to the will of Allah. Mohammed said the chief duty of man is to submit to the will of Allah.

Third, he said there is coming a great and terrible day of judgment in which God will raise up the dead to life and will judge them and reward them, based upon their deeds. Those who were found worthy would be given to a wonderful, sensuous life in heaven, and those who do not make it will be condemned to hell.

The majority of the people in Mecca did not think too highly of this new prophet or his revelations. They began to criticize and attack him. In 622 A.D. he fled to Medina, about 280 miles north of Mecca. This was the beginning of Islam.

CHAPTER FOURTEEN

The New Age of Islam Begins

In the Middle East, everything is based upon the time when Mohammed fled to Medina in 622 A.D. That was the beginning of their calendar; zero, in the Muslim calendar.

It was in Medina that he first tried to get the Christians and Jews who were living there to follow him as "the prophet." He called himself a prophet and an apostle, although that term was not used in their culture.

He used the term "prophet" to appeal to the Jews and "apostle" to appeal to the Christians. He told them, interestingly, to pray to Jerusalem. When they did not accept him as a prophet or an apostle, he then rejected them and told the other people to pray to Mecca to Allah, his tribal deity.

He then began to receive more revelations. It is very interesting what these revelations were. He received revelations that he was to loot and steal from caravans that were going through the region. That call from Allah drew a rag-tailed crew of followers.

There were many cases where Mohammed and his followers would loot and rob caravans and would kill all the men in order to satisfy his greed. In fact, the Koran and history reports that he fought over sixty-six such battles, killing tens of thousands.

In one of his revelations, he was told to kill and drive out all the Jews. On one occasion, he had one thousand Jewish men brought together and had them all beheaded. Islam became known as the religion of the sword. Beheading is still the demonstration of Islamic power over all infidels.

In 628 A.D., Mohammed received a revelation that Islam was to be exalted above all other religions, including Christianity and Judaism.

By 629 A.D. Mohammed had raised up an army of ten thousand men. He returned to Mecca, where he had been cast out, and conquered it. By force, he imposed Islam on the rest of the Arabian tribes. He died in 632 A.D. having conquered much of the Arabian Peninsula.

Islam then spread, by the sword, across North Africa, and for fourteen centuries has continued converting by the sword in its reign of terror and intimidation.

CHAPTER FIFTEEN
Sharia Law

Much has been said about *shariah,* or sharia law, without actually understanding the details of this oppressive system. In the United States, many pocket areas of non-engaging Muslims demand that they be under sharia law instead of the American system of laws. They demand that they be left alone, and stand in defiance to the American Justice system.

They refuse to integrate into the American society, which in most cases is giving them vast amounts of financial "assistance" and free health and educational provision. Many see their actions as a kind of stealth jihad toward sharia dominance in this country.

A Look at Sharia Law
Sharia law includes the following:

- *Hygiene and purification laws*, including the manner of cleansing, either wudhu or ghusl.

- *Economic laws*, including Zakat, the annual *almsgiving*; Waqf, the religious endowment; the prohibition on interest, or Riba; as well as *inheritance laws*.

- *Dietary laws* including Dhabihah, or ritual slaughter.

- *Theological obligations*, including the Hajj or pilgrimage, with its rituals such as Tawaf, Sa'yee and the Stoning of the Devil; Salat, formal worship; Salat al-Janazah, the funeral prayer; and celebrating Eid al-Adha.

- *Marital jurisprudence*, including Nikah, the marriage contract; and *divorce*, known as Khula if initiated by a woman.

- *Criminal jurisprudence*, including Hudud, fixed punishments; Tazir, discretionary punishment; Qisas, or retaliation; Diyya, or blood money; and *apostasy*.

- *Military jurisprudence*, including *jus in bello* and *casus belli*; Hudna, or truce; and rules regarding *prisoners of war*.

- *Dress code*, including *hijab*; man and children's clothing and dress codes within the home and marital bedroom.

Of all legal systems in the world today, sharia law is the most intrusive and restrictive, especially against women. According to sharia law[17]:

- Theft is punishable by amputation of the right hand (above).

- Criticizing or denying any part of the Quran is punishable by death.

- Criticizing Muhammad or denying that he is a prophet is punishable by death.

- Criticizing or denying Allah, the god of Islam, is punishable by death.

- A Muslim who becomes a non-Muslim is punishable by death.

- A non-Muslim who leads a Muslim away from Islam is punishable by death.

- A non-Muslim man who marries a Muslim woman is punishable by death.

---

17 www.billionbibles.org/sharia/sharia-law.html

- A man can marry an infant girl and consummate the marriage when she is *9 years old*.

- A girl's clitoris should be cut. (Muhammad's words, Book 41, Kitab Al-Adab, Hadith 5251)

- A woman can have one husband, who can have up to four wives; Muhammad can have more.

- A man can beat his wife for insubordination.

- A man can unilaterally divorce his wife; a woman needs her husband's consent to divorce.

- A divorced wife loses custody of all children over six years of age, or when they exceed it.

- Testimonies of four male witnesses are required to prove rape against a woman.

- A woman who has been raped cannot testify in court against her rapist(s).

- A woman's testimony in court, allowed in property cases, carries one-half the weight of a man's.

- A female heir inherits half of what a male heir inherits.

- A woman cannot drive a car, as it leads to *fitnah* (upheaval).

- A woman cannot speak alone to a man who is not her husband or relative.

- Meat to eat must come from animals that have been sacrificed to Allah (i.e., be *"Halal"*).

- Muslims should engage in *Taqiyya* and lie to non-Muslims to advance Islam.

CHAPTER SIXTEEN

The Six Beliefs of Islam

God: There is one true God, named Allah.

Angels: They are the servants of God, through whom he reveals his will. The greatest angel is Gabriel, who appeared to Mohammed. Everyone has two "recording angels": one to record their good deeds, the other to record their bad deeds.

The Prophets: Allah has spoken through many prophets, but the final and greatest of these is Mohammed. Other prophets include Noah, Abraham, Moses, and Jesus.

The Holy Books: The Koran or Qur'an is the holiest book of Islam, believed to be Allah's final revelation to man, and it supersedes all previous revelations, including the Bible. It contains Allah's word as passed on orally to Mohammed by Gabriel. It contains 114 chapters, or Suras, also called Surahs.

The Koran is considered pure and without error. Muslims also recognize the Law of Moses, the Psalms, and the gospels, but consider them to be badly corrupted.

The Hadith, or Sunnah, contains the recorded sayings and deeds of the prophet Mohammed. It is second only to the Koran and is often used to clarify things not clear in the Koran.

The Day of Judgment: A terrible day on which each person's good and bad deeds will be balanced to determine his fate. Muslims will go to paradise, and all nonbelievers and Muslims who did not maintain their faith and good works will go to hell. There is no original sin. All of mankind starts out sinless, thus the need for a final judgment.

The Decree of God: Allah ordains the fate of all. Muslims are fatalistic. "If Allah wills it" is the comment of a devout Muslim on almost every situation or decision he faces.

CHAPTER SEVENTEEN

The Five Pillars of Islam

1. **Affirmation**: "There is no God but Allah, and Mohammed is his messenger." This is recited constantly by devout Muslims.

2. **The Fast:** Faithful Muslims fast from dawn to dusk every day during the ninth month of the Islamic calendar, Ramadan, which is sacred.

3. **Almsgiving:** A worthy Muslim must give 2.5% of his income to the poor.

4. **Prayer:** Muslims are required to pray five times a day, kneeling and facing Mecca.

5. **The Pilgrimage:** Muslims are expected to journey to Mecca at least once in their lifetime.

CHAPTER EIGHTEEN

Islam and Christianity Compared

Islam is one of those "other gospels" that Paul warned us about time and again. In Chapter 11 of Second Corinthians, Paul warns us that Satan himself transforms himself into an angel of light. Islam teaches that while Allah is known by ninety-nine names, he is so far above man in every way that he is virtually unknowable. Allah will send individuals to Paradise or Hell, as they deserve, and as he chooses.

> Absolute monotheism is the core presupposition of Islam. The doctrine of tawhid (oneness) in Islam states that Allah is utterly transcendent (Quran 112:1-4). In other words, He is not just monotheistic but a wholly distinct, unique, indivisible, and completely separate (impersonal) being who is unknowable by "personal" beings like us. Allah exists without a place, independent of creation, with no resemblance to his creations.

Nothing in all of creation can be compared to Allah.

This central doctrine of tawhid creates an interesting logical challenge. How can one know anything about something that is unknowable?

The Hadith, or tradition attributed to Muhammad, also teaches that Allah has ninety-nine names that describe various aspects of Allah's nature and personalities. If Allah is unknowable, then how can we attribute ninety-nine names to him and make him known?

The Bible, in contrast, reveals that God is personal, and He has revealed Himself in the Bible so that He can be known. In fact, the Bible teaches that God created mankind for the express purpose of knowing Him personally.[18]

What the Koran Says About Jesus

He was not the Son of God.

"And the Jews say: Uzair is the son of Allah; and the Christians say: The Messiah is the son of Allah; these are the words of their mouths; they imitate the saying of those who disbelieved before; may Allah destroy them; how they are turned away!"

Sura 9:30

---

18 answersingenesis.org/world-religions/islams-view-of-god-and-his-revelation/

He was not divine.

"Certainly they disbelieve who say: Surely, Allah – He is the Messiah, son of Marium. Say: Who then could control anything as against Allah when He wished to destroy the Messiah son of Marium and his mother and all those on the earth? And Allah's is the kingdom of the heavens and the earth and what is between them; He creates what He pleases; and Allah has power over all things."

Sura 5.17

"The Messiah, son of Marium is but an apostle; apostles before him have indeed passed away; and his mother was a truthful woman; they both used to eat food. See how we make the communications clear to them, then behold, how they are turned away."

Sura 5.75

He was not crucified.

"And their saying: Surely we have killed the Messiah, Isa son of Marium, the apostle of Allah; and they did not kill him nor did they crucify him, but it appeared to them so (like Isa) and most surely those who differ therein are only in a doubt about it; they have no knowledge respecting it, but only follow a conjecture, and they killed him not for sure."

Sura 4.157

"Nay! Allah took him up to Himself; and Allah is Mighty, Wise."

Sura 4.15

He did not atone for our sins.

"On the day when the earth shall be changed into a different earth, and the heavens (as well), and they shall come forth before Allah, the One, the Supreme. And you will see the guilty on that day linked together in chains. Their shirts made of pitch and the fire covering their faces. That Allah may requite each soul (according to) what it has earned; surely Allah is swift in reckoning."

Sura 14.48-51

He will return, but His Second Coming to be a witness for Mohammed.

"And there is not one of the followers of the Book but most certainly believes in this before his death, and on the day of resurrection he (Isa) shall be a witness against them."

Sura 4.159

He is not God come in the flesh, the "son" of God.

"O followers of the Book! Do not exceed the limits in your religion, and do not speak (lies) against Allah, but (speak) the truth; the Messiah, Isa son of Marium is only an apostle of Allah and His Word which He communicated to Marium and a spirit from Him; believe therefore in Allah and His apostles, and say not, Three. Desist, it is better for you; Allah is only one God; far be it from His glory that He should have a son, whatever is in the heavens and whatever is in the earth is His, and Allah is sufficient for a Protector."

Sura 4.171

There is no Trinity.

"Certainly they disbelieve who say: Surely Allah is the third (person) of the three; and there is no god but the one God, and if they desist not from what they say, a painful chastisement shall befall those among them who disbelieve."

Sura 5.73

What the Bible Says About Jesus

"In the beginning was the Word, and the Word was with God, and the Word was God. He was with God in the beginning. Through him all things were made; without him nothing was made that has been made. In him was life, and that life was the light of men."

John 1:1-4

"The Word became flesh and made his dwelling among us. We have seen his glory, the glory of the One and Only, who came from the Father, full of grace and truth."

John 1:14

"For God so loved the world that he gave his one and only Son, that whoever believes in him shall not perish but have eternal life."

John 3:16

"Jesus answered, 'I am the way and the truth and the life. No one comes to the Father except through me.'"

John 14:6

"Dear friends, do not believe every spirit, but test the spirits to see whether they are from God, because many false prophets have gone out into the world.

This is how you can recognize the Spirit of God: Every spirit that acknowledges that Jesus Christ has come in the flesh is from God, but every spirit that does not acknowledge Jesus is not from God. This is the spirit of the antichrist, which you have heard is coming and even now is already in the world."

1 John 4:1-3

"For in Christ all the fullness of the Deity lives in bodily form."

Colossians 2:9

"This is my blood of the covenant, which is poured out for many for the forgiveness of sins."

Matthew 26:28

"When he had received the drink, Jesus said, 'It is finished.' With that, he bowed his head and gave up his spirit."

John 19:30

"Many of the Jews read this sign, for the place where Jesus was crucified was near the city, and the sign was written in Aramaic, Latin and Greek."

John 19:20

"In the past God spoke to our forefathers through the prophets at many times and in various ways, but in these last days he has spoken to us by his Son, whom he appointed heir of all things, and through whom he made the universe. The Son is the radiance of God's glory and the exact representation of his being, sustaining all things by his powerful word. After he had provided purification for sins, he sat down at the right hand of the Majesty in heaven."

Hebrews 1:1-3

CHAPTER NINETEEN

Is Allah the God of Abraham, Isaac, and Jacob?

According to the Koran, Allah chose Hagar and her son, Ishmael, for his covenant. But just because Mohammed said it, doesn't make it so! The God of the Bible chose Abraham's other son, Isaac, as heir to His covenant. This act has forever separated the two, and the people of Ishmael have warred against the children of Isaac ever since.

> *"And the Angel of the LORD said to her (Hagar): 'Behold, you are with child, and you shall bear a son. You shall call his name Ishmael, because the LORD has heard your affliction. He shall be a wild man; his hand shall be against every man, and every man's hand against him. And he shall dwell in the presence of all his brethren.'"*
>
> Genesis 16:11-12

> *"And Abraham said to God, 'If only Ishmael might live under your blessing!" Then God said, "Yes, but*

> *your wife Sarah will bear you a son, and you will call him Isaac. I will establish my covenant with him as an everlasting covenant for his descendants after him.*
>
> *'And as for Ishmael, I have heard you: I will surely bless him; I will make him fruitful and will greatly increase his numbers. He will be the father of twelve rulers, and I will make him into a great nation.*
>
> *'But my covenant I will establish with Isaac, whom Sarah will bear to you by this time next year.' When he had finished speaking with Abraham, God went up from him."*
>
> Genesis 17:18-22

Allah is an impersonal being, impossible to approach or comprehend. The God of the Bible befriends men like Abraham (Isaiah 41:8) and talks with them (Genesis 18:23-33)!

Allah is a god of fear and terrorism that commands destruction upon those who refuse to convert to Islam.

The God of the Bible delights to show His boundless mercy. His gospel is the "Good News" of peace and forgiveness. He tells us to love our enemies, not kill them.

Allah requires total obedience to Islam and weighs the works of people. Allah and the Koran relegate Jesus to simply being the last prophet before Mohammed, below his authority. Jesus was not the Way, and could only point the way to Mohammed.

The Bible clearly states that Jesus was, and still is, the only Way to the Father.

Allah required the works of Mohammed to complete his words of judgment to man.

The God of the Bible sent His son who did the finished work of grace for man.

Allah requires that the sons of men must die for him.

The God of the Bible sent His son to die for us.

In the light of Allah's actual origin, and the radical differences between Allah and the God of the Bible, we must conclude that Allah is not God; nor is the name, Allah, a generic Mid-East name for the biblical God, as even many Christians think.

Allah is the name of a demonic, false god, a pagan stone idol that cannot save anyone from anything. Rather, through his false prophet, Mohammed, hundreds of millions continue to be led into eternal darkness.

CHAPTER TWENTY
Islam and Freemasonry

Most people, including the Masons involved with it, do not realize the deep spiritual ties between Islam and Freemasonry. Most Masons get involved with the Lodge out of peer pressure; their friends are in it, their grandfather was in it, or some get involved in it for business reasons. They see Freemasonry as a way to progress in their business and social lives.

The secret, mystic rituals and symbolism of Freemasonry attract others. Most of us have seen Masons like the Shriners parading around in their red fezzes riding their funny cars in parades when the Shrine Circus comes to town.

People wonder, "Well, what about the Shriners? We hear about the Shriners' Hospitals, about Masonic homes for Masons, about all the good works they do. Every Masonic Lodge has its various local charities. Just in California, the California Masonic Foundation and other Masonic-affiliated organizations award more than one million dollars in scholarships to students every year. Everyone knows about the Shrine Circus and the many people who are helped by the money raised. What is not well advertised is that the majority of its income goes to the organization and its internal programs.

We are often asked, *"Why are you criticizing them? Are you saying that they have something to hide from the world?"*

Yes, we are saying *just* that. This is clearly the case with the Shriners. Their public image is that of a fun time group pouring out millions of dollars into charity, all the while dressed up in a party spirit, wearing their red fezzes with great aplomb.

Let me explain what actually happens when the Shriners go through their sacred initiation ritual and place themselves under the spiritual headship of the Muslim god, Allah.

In usual occult fashion, the initiate swears that he will be inseparably obligated to this "most powerful and binding oath" in advance, and that he may NEVER retract or depart from it. Let me quote from several actual Shriners' initiation rituals.

The God of The Mystic Shrine

The candidates for this ritual kneel at the ALTAR OF OBLIGATION with arms bound, leaning upon the top, heads bowed.

There they are required to "assume a most powerful and binding oath, inseparably uniting yourself with us, and once taken, it can never be retracted or departed from."

The oath itself is curse enough, being four pages in length. Its penalty included "having my eyeballs pierced to the center with a three-edged blade."

The revelation of truth is in the candidates' sealing of the oath, revealing the true nature of the Masonic god of the "Mystic Shrine":

> "...and may ALLAH, the god of Arab, Moslem and Mohammedan, the GOD OF OUR FATHERS, support me to the entire fulfillment of the same, Amen, Amen, Amen."[19]

The late Muslim Leader, Elijah Muhammad, spiritual leader of the nation's Black Muslims, understood the true Islamic roots of Freemasonry. He was quoted in *When the Word is Given*:

> Here in America there are also three and one half million indirect believers in Islam, in the secret order called the Shriners, or higher Masons... You are no longer called a Mason. You are then called a Moslem Son, and in that order you are taught the prayers of the Moslems and you come under the teachings of Islam.[20]

---

19 *The Ancient Arabic Order, Nobles of the Mystic Shrine*, pages 35-39, Allen Publishing Co. New York, NY, and *The Mystic Shrine, An Illustrated Ritual of the Ancient Arabic Order Nobles of the Shrine*, 1975 edition, (pages 20-22).
20 Louis Lomax, 1963, 1st edition, page 124.

After a man passes through the "Blue Lodge," or the first three degrees of Masonry, and has achieved the status of Master Mason, he can petition to become a member of the Shrine or the "Ancient Arabic Order of the Nobles of the Mystic Shrine." Until 2000, one had to complete the Scottish Rite, or York Rite, degrees of Masonry to be eligible for Shrine membership, but now any Master Mason can join.

One of the most distinguishing marks of a Shriner is the fez hat that he wears. So named after the city of Fez, Morocco – which by the way has been the site of numerous documented massacres of both Jews and Christians by various Muslim conquerors – the Fez is a distinctly Muslim symbol and, at least indirectly, celebrates the Muslim conquest of the area. Its emblems are uniquely Islamic in their design and meaning.

The emblem found on the fez is that of Muslim origin. It contains the Arabic pagan god symbols of the Crescent Moon and Star, originally the symbol of the Ottoman Empire, now an international symbol of Islam. The symbols are hung under a "scimitar," or an Arabic sword of war. This is the sword that has killed the "infidels" down through the ages under Muslim conquest.

Situated in the middle of the moon symbol is the Sphinx. This represents the Great Sphinx of Egypt that has its roots thoroughly in ancient Egyptian paganism and demonic symbolism. The word *sphinx* means "the strangler," or as it is more widely used in Arabic, "The Father of Terror." Perhaps this symbolizes that Allah truly is the "father of terror?"

It is often explained that the color red represents the blood of Christians and Jews spilled by the Muslim conquerors. I can find no hard facts to back this claim, but it is a fact that the fez is a Muslim symbol.

The below excerpt about the Fez is from a Shriner Website:

Why Shriners wear a Fez

> The red fez with a black tassel, the Shrine's most distinctive symbol, has been handed down through the ages. It derives its name from the place where it was first manufactured – the *holy* city of Fez, Morocco. The fez was chosen as part of the *Shrine's Arabic theme*, around which the color and pageantry of the Shrine are developed."[21]

Again, let me quote from another source regarding the cultic, Islamic core of the Shrine.

> The Shriner meets in a "TEMPLE" – most of which have distinctly Arabic names. They are often built to resemble a Mosque. He wears his fez with the Muslim symbols on it. He takes his oaths and says his prayers in the name of ALLAH. Many of his secret passwords and code phrases are in Arabic, which he is required to memorize in order to be in the "order."

---

21 www.amranshriners.us/history.html

Candidates for induction into the Shriners are greeted by a [Masonic] High Priest, who says: *"By the existence of Allah and the creed of Mohammed; by the legendary sanctity of our Tabernacle at Mecca, we greet you."*

The inductees then swear on the Bible and the Koran, in the name of Mohammed, and invoke Masonry's usual gruesome penalties upon themselves:

"I do hereby, upon this Bible, and on the mysterious legend of the Koran, and its dedication to the Mohammedan faith, promise and swear and vow that I will never reveal any secret part or portion whatsoever of the ceremonies and now upon this sacred book, by the sincerity of a Moslem's oath I here register this irrevocable vow in willful violation whereof may I incur the fearful penalty of having my eyeballs pierced to the center with a three-edged blade, my feet flayed, and I be forced to walk the hot sands upon the sterile shores of the Red Sea until the flaming sun shall strike me with livid plague, and may Allah, the god of Arab, Moslem, and Mohammedan, the god of our fathers, support me to the entire fulfillment of the same. Amen. Amen. Amen."

With this oath, Christians swear on the Koran, and declare Allah to be "the god of our fathers."

From the perspective of Christianity and Islam alike, Shriners take the name of God in vain, and mock both faiths.[22]

Freemasonry is a puzzle to the uninitiated public. It appears to be a quaint society designed to bring fellowship and benevolence together in a fraternal manner, yet its secret side makes many people more than a bit wary, with good reason.

This is clearly the case with the Shriners. Their public image is that of a fun-time group pouring out millions of dollars into charity, all the while dressed up in their red fezzes in a party spirit.

Again, let me be clear that the fez itself is an example of this double meaning behind most of Freemasonry's facade. Worn and even carried to the grave with pompous dignity, the history of the fez is barbaric and anti-Christian.

As I mentioned before, in the early 8th century, Muslim hordes overran the Moroccan city of Fez, shouting, *"There is no god but Allah and Mohammed is his prophet,"* or *"Allahu Akbar."*

It is the warlike declaration that Allah and Islam are dominant over every other form of government, religion, law, or ethic, which is why Islamic jihadists in the midst of killing infidels so often shout it in order to strike terror in the hearts of the enemies of Allah.[23]

---

22 Penn, Lee, *The Origins and Influence of Masonry*, SCP Journal Vol. 25:2-25:3 2001.
23 www.breitbart.com/immigration/2015/12/25/allahu-akbar-means-almost-everything-except-establishment-media-says

As the Muslim hordes swarmed over Fez, they butchered approximately fifty thousand Christians. These men, women, and children were slain because of their faith in Christ, all in the name of Allah, the same demon god to whom every Shriner must bow, with hands tied behind his back, in worship, proclaiming him the god of his fathers in the Shrine initiation, at the Altar of Obligation.

The Shriners' blood oath and confession of Allah as God is documented in the secret Lodge document. Remember that Allah is not just another name for God. Allah is the name of *another* god. In usual occult fashion, the initiate swears that he will be inseparably obligated to this "most powerful and binding oath" and that he may NEVER retract or depart from it.

During the butchering of the people of Fez, the streets literally ran red with the blood of the martyred Christians. The Muslim murderers dipped their caps in the blood of their victims as a testimony to Allah. These bloodstained caps eventually were called fezzes and became a badge of honor for those who killed a Christian. The Shriners wear that same red fez today. The greatest tragedy is that men who profess to be Christians themselves often wear the fez.

It must cause God to weep.

CHAPTER TWENTY-ONE

It's a Mystery to Me

It is a real mystery to me how the Islamic world perceives Jesus.

In Islam, they are told he was born of God, not man; that he lived a pure and sinless life, was not crucified, but raised to heaven and shall come again to proclaim Mohammed the greatest prophet and Islam the true faith.

He will tell the entire world that he was really here to proclaim the coming of Mohammed. He will say that the Jews, his disciples, and all of Christendom have been wrong for two thousand years, and we must all convert to Islam to be righteous before Allah and go to that Islamic heaven.

Yet, if we follow this through, we come to some strange conclusions.

1. If what they say about his birth, life, ministry, and bodily accession to heaven are true, then we have to ask why this would be. If the second part of this picture is true – his submission to Mohammed, the one mightier than he – why would he say so many things like:

> *"I am the way and the truth and the life. No one comes to the Father except through me."*
>
> John 14:6

> *"I and My Father are one." Then the Jews took up stones again to stone Him.*
>
> John 10:30-31

2. Why would he foretell his death on the cross and his resurrection from death? Either the Koran is wrong, or the Bible is wrong and Jesus was a liar. If he was a liar, how could the Koran say he lived a sinless life and was lifted up to heaven by God?

There can be no compromise in such a black or white issue. He was either who he said he was, or the greatest liar in history. The Muslims cannot have it both ways in such a basic matter. A thing cannot "be" and "not be" at the same time.

3. If the Muslim view of Christ were true, why would we read about John being the proclaimer of the coming Christ, when we should be reading about Jesus proclaiming the coming of Mohammed? (Some Islamic scholars interpret verses foretelling the coming of the Holy Spirit to mean the coming of Mohammed).

4. If Mohammed was the greater prophet, why was Jesus (the liar) lifted up to heaven and Mohammed left to die and be buried like every other man?

I am reminded of the scripture in Psalm 82 where the unrighteous rulers and judges were rebuked for their evil doings and self-exaltation:

> They do not know, nor do they understand; they walk about in darkness; all the foundations of the earth are unstable. I said, "You are gods, and all of you are children of the Most High. But you shall die like men, and fall like one of the princes."

CHAPTER TWENTY-TWO

Jesus and Mohammed

Even in Islamic doctrine, some key issues of the lives of Christ and Mohammed do not make sense. Jesus was born of God, by a virgin, Mohammed was born of man; Jesus lived a life of purity, without sin, history shows that Mohammed did not. He married, had concubines, and even took a child as a wife.

Jesus turned water to wine, fed the five thousand; he healed the sick, opened blind eyes, cleansed the lepers, raised his friend Lazarus from the dead, walked on water, quieted the raging sea. He taught his disciples to operate in these gifts and gave the power of the Holy Spirit to all believers.

Mohammed did none of these things. He raised no one from the dead. He healed no one. In fact he and his followers robbed, raped, murdered, and slaughtered many.

Jesus condemned stealing: "Thou shall not steal" (Matthew 19:18); but, Mohammed called for stealing from unbelievers: *"The people felt hungry and captured [stole] some camels and sheep"* (Bukhari 44:668).

Mohammed told his people to lie to unbelievers (Sahih Muslim 6303, Bukhari 49:857) but Jesus reminded his followers to be truthful: "Thou shalt not bear false witness" (Matthew 19:18).

Jesus' tomb was empty. He was raised from the grave to heaven, and sits on the right hand of the Father. He is our intercessor.

Mohammed died a man. It is said that he died from what appears to have been syphilis. He was buried as any other man was buried. He never rose from the grave. He does not intercede for mankind. He is just dead and buried.

Jesus will fulfill his prophetic promise of coming again and the Christian world awaits His soon coming. Mohammed never suggested that he would return, and not a single Muslim awaits it. Could they be any more different?

CHAPTER TWENTY-THREE

The Holy Jihad – A Way of Life and Death

In 2001, as many as 350 Muslim religious scholars gathered for a meeting in Baghdad and confirmed in the strongest terms the legitimacy of Islamic martyrdom operations one of the highest forms of Jihad (The House of War, or non-Muslim) against oppression.

After three days of deliberations, it is reported that these scholars unanimously concluded that Muslim Mujahideen, or freedom fighters, who blow themselves up at enemy targets, are not suicidal but are bona fide heroic martyrs whose acts are totally compatible with Islamic teachings.

"It is the duty of every Muslim facing overwhelming and brutal aggression, as is the case in Palestine, to confront this oppression with all available means," said the scholars in their edict.

The edict reaffirmed previous edicts by such prominent Islamic jurists as Sheikh Yousef al-Qaradawi, who ruled that freedom fighters who detonate explosives strapped to themselves sacrifice their lives to attack the "enemies of God and Islam."

"The people of Palestine have been forced into a situation where they must choose between dying as martyr-bombers or slaughtered like sheep at the hands of a nefarious enemy. Dying as martyr-bombers in this case is considered a very sublime form of Jihad," said the edict.

Martyrdom operations, which "the Jewish-controlled media in the U.S. and Europe refer to as suicide bomb attacks," have attracted overwhelming support among Muslim theologians, particularly after Palestinian Islamist leaders explained that martyrdom operations were the only means to make the Jews refrain from perpetrating a large-scale holocaust against Palestinian civilians.

Not long after, the U.S. exerted behind-the-curtain pressure on the Saudi government to instruct the Saudi religious establishment to issue edicts opposing martyrdom operations. However, while the Saudis, vastly rich from the oil money the U.S. pours out to them in abundance, only smiled nicely and rejected the idea.

Saudi scholars rejected this American pressure, describing American intervention in "Islamic theological matters as brazen and shameless."[24]

I would like to share this excellent statement I received about Muslims and America:[25]

---

24 The Palestinian Times, on Line, October 2001 Report
25 While the original source unavailable, the content is correct and verifiable.

Can Muslims Be Good Americans and Live in Peace Among Christian and Jews?

Theologically – No. Because his allegiance is to Allah, the moon god of Arabia.

Religiously – No. Because no other religion is accepted by Allah except Islam (Quran 2:256).

Scripturally – No. Because his allegiance is to the five Pillars of Islam and the Quran.

Socially – No. Because his allegiance to Islam forbids him to make friends with Christians or Jews.

Politically – No. Because he must submit to the mullahs (spiritual leaders), who teach annihilation of Israel and destruction of America, the great Satan.

Domestically – No. Because he is instructed to marry four women, and beat and scourge his wife when she disobeys him (Quran 4:34).

Intellectually – No. Because he cannot accept the American Constitution since it is based on Biblical principles, and he believes the Bible to be corrupt.

Philosophically – No. Because Islam, Muhammad, and the Quran does not allow freedom of religion and expression. Democracy and Islam cannot co-exist. Every Muslim government is either dictatorial or autocratic.

Spiritually – No. Because when we declare "one nation under God," the Christian's God is loving and kind, while Allah is NEVER referred to as Heavenly father, nor is he ever called love in the Quran's ninety-nine excellent names.

CHAPTER TWENTY-FOUR

A Holy War Fought to the Death without Compromise

The *jihad* is a holy war; one fought to the death – a great and noble death honoring Allah in the defense of the faith. Those Muslim men who die as martyrs of the faith receive immediate entrance to heaven, where they are given many virgins and opulent mansions filled with wealth and servants for their great gift to the cause of Allah.

This firm doctrine of holy martyrdom results in the justification for slaying anyone who will not live the peace of Islam, those who have brought strife against the children of Allah, or who resist the mighty movement of the great world of Islam.

> You who believe! Shall I guide you to a commerce that will save you from a painful torment? That you believe in Allah and His Messenger and that

> you strive hard and fight in the Cause of Allah with your wealth and your lives, that will be better for you, if you but know! (If you do so) He will forgive you your sins, and admit you into Gardens under which rivers flow, and pleasant dwelling in Gardens of Eternity, that is indeed the great success.
>
> Sura 61:10-12

Islamic clerics by the scores proclaimed on television that the jihad and destruction such as seen on September 11, 2001, was not part of the Muslim faith. They spoke about "The Peace of Islam," or "The Peace of Allah," terms that sound fine in simple English, but actually mean being at peace by converting and bowing to Allah alone or dying by their hand.

Anyone outside that narrow definition is among the infidels. American leaders, even many Christian leaders, smiled at them, nodding in agreement to something they did not understand.

Unfortunately, the jihad is a very real, core element of the Islamic faith. It is also a doctrinal teaching that has led to the deaths of millions of Muslims throughout history.

Let's look at the Holy Jihad being waged against Europe and America. It is not just a single group of militants. That would make our work easy. This jihad is operating across the entire world of Islam and draws its fanatics from every corner of the faith.

It's latest tactic in Europe and the United States is to use small groups and mostly young single males; radical

A HOLY WAR FOUGHT TO THE DEATH WITHOUT COMPROMISE

jihadists who slip through the cracks without too much effort. The December 2, 2015, Islamic jihadist terrorist attack in San Bernardino was an example of this tactic. Syed Rizwan Farook and Tashfeen Malik attacked Farook's office holiday party, killing fourteen and wounding twenty-two. They were later killed in a shootout with police.

What many described as the deadliest Islamic terrorist attack on American soil since the 9/11 attack in New York took place in Orlando, Florida, on June 12, 2016.

A lone gunman, pledging loyalty to ISIS, killed forty-nine people and injured fifty-three others inside Pulse, a gay nightclub in Orlando. The gunman, Omar Mir Seddique Mateen, was heard shouting "Allah Akbar" during the episode.

ISIS later praised him and took credit for the attacks, promising more to come. This was ISIS, and the violent jihad, come to American shores.

Earlier attacks hit Europe hard:

> On the evening of November 13, 2015, a series of coordinated terrorist attacks occurred in Paris, France, and in Saint Denis, the city's northern suburb, beginning at 21:20, three suicide bombers struck near the Stade de France in Saint-Denis, followed by suicide bombings and mass shootings at cafés, restaurants, and a music venue in central Paris.
>
> The attackers killed 130 people, including eighty-nine at the Batacian theatre where they took hostages before engaging in a standoff with

police. Another 368 people were injured, eighty to ninety-nine seriously. Seven of the attackers also died, while the authorities continued to search for accomplices. The attacks were the deadliest on France since World War II, and the deadliest in the European Union since the Madrid train bombings in 2004.

France had been on high alert since the January 2015 attacks on the *Charlie Hebdo* offices and a Jewish supermarket in Paris that killed seventeen people and wounded twenty-two, including civilians and police officers.

The Islamic State of Iraq and the Levant [ISIL] claimed responsibility for the attacks, saying that it was retaliation for the French airstrikes on ISIL targets in Syria and Iraq.

The President of France, Francois Hollande, said the attacks were an act of war by ISIL planned in Syria, organized in Belgium, and perpetrated with help from citizens of France. All of the known Paris attackers were EU citizens who had fought in Syria. Some of them had returned to Europe among the flow of migrants and refugees.[26]

I was exchanging emails with several Muslims as I worked through this report, and in discussing the attempt to separate Islam out from the terrorist attacks, one scoffed at such an idea. He wrote:

---

26 en.wikipedia.org/wiki/November_2015_Paris_attacks

A HOLY WAR FOUGHT TO THE DEATH WITHOUT COMPROMISE

> Islam does not compartmentalize life into the so-called sacred and secular. Get this clear. All of life is one unit.

Not clear enough? In Islam, it is not possible to disentangle the spiritual from the political, or the cultural from the economic. Islam is the path of unification and a total way of life. Everything that Muslims do must be unified with Islam.

Hal Lindsey is one of the most knowledgeable Christians on this subject, having studied Islam and Muslims for many years. In one daily commentary at his web site, he had this to say on September 17, 2001:

> The enemy we face is far more than a certain country, or a certain race. It is multi-national and multiracial. The enemy is found all over the world disguised in many clever guises. The enemy is organized into cell groups that can operate autonomously or can be joined into multi-cell strike groups, as on September the 11th.
>
> The enemy is fanatical and totally dedicated to the common goal of destroying the U.S.A. and Israel. Our enemy has been created by one common all consuming core-Islam. Our enemy is blindly courageous because of the teachings of his religious leaders that when he dies attacking the enemy, he goes immediately to paradise to be given seventy beautiful virgins for his heavenly harem.
>
> Our enemy will therefore gladly volunteer to give his life in a suicide attack against the U.S.A.

and its people. All the forces of Fundamental Islam have not just declared war on the U.S.A.; they have declared a "jihad or holy war" against us. This Jihad has been strengthened with many "fatwahs," which give specific, murderous and explicit religious commands to kill all Americans in every place and by any means possible.

Osama Bin Laden issued such a fatwah in which he declared it to be the sacred duty to Allah for all Muslims to kill Americans at every opportunity by any means. Specifically, his fatwah ordered:

> "We with God's help call on every Muslim who believes in God [Allah] and wishes to be rewarded to comply with God's [Allah's] order to kill the Americans and plunder their money wherever and whenever they find it."

When Osama Bin Laden was taken out, it upped the game tremendously. Now we face endless Bin Laden types, on every continent.

But make note of who the enemy was to Bin Laden, and still is to all his follow-on martyrs. It isn't the United States. It isn't the government. It is each and every individual American – ordinary Americans like those who now lie entombed under a million tons of rubble in Manhattan. It's you.

CHAPTER TWENTY-FIVE

Terrorism is All About Islam

Salman Rushdie has been on a death list ever since he wrote a less-than-spiritual book about his faith. He has been in hiding for many years now. These are some of his comments about this holy war that "isn't a holy war." They are excerpted from an article published by him in *The New York Times*, on November 2, 2001.

> LONDON – "This isn't about Islam." The world's leaders have been repeating this mantra for weeks, partly in the virtuous hope of deterring reprisal attacks on innocent Muslims living in the West, partly because if the United States is to maintain its coalition against terror it can't afford to suggest that Islam and terrorism are in any way related.
>
> The trouble with this necessary disclaimer is that it isn't true. If this isn't about Islam, why the worldwide Muslim demonstrations in support of Osama bin Laden and Al Qaeda and now ISIS?

Why did those ten thousand men armed with swords and axes mass on the Pakistan-Afghanistan frontier, answering some mullah's call to jihad? Why are the war's first British casualties three Muslim men who died fighting on the Taliban side?

Why the routine anti-Semitism of the much repeated Islamic slander that "the Jews" arranged the hits on the World Trade Center and the Pentagon, with the oddly self-deprecating explanation offered by the Taliban leadership, among others, that Muslims could not have the technological know-how or organizational sophistication to pull off such a feat?

Why does Imran Khan, the Pakistani ex-sports star turned politician, demand to be shown the evidence of Al Qaeda's guilt while apparently turning a deaf ear to the self-incriminating statements of Al Qaeda's own spokesmen (there will be a rain of aircraft from the skies, Muslims in the West are warned not to live or work in tall buildings)? Why all the talk about American military infidels desecrating the sacred soil of Saudi Arabia if some sort of definition of what is sacred is not at the heart of the present discontents?

Of course this is "about Islam." The question is, what exactly does that mean? After all, most religious belief isn't very theological. Most Muslims are not profound Koranic analysts. For a vast number of "believing" Muslim men, "Islam" stands, in a jumbled, half-examined way, not only for the fear of God – the fear more than the love, one suspects – but also for a cluster of customs, opinions, and prejudices that include their dietary practices; the sequestration or near-sequestration of "their" women; the sermons delivered by their mullahs of choice; a loathing of modern society in general, riddled as it is with music, godlessness, and sex; and a more particularized loathing (and fear) of the prospect that their own immediate surroundings could be taken over – "Westoxicated" – by the liberal Western-style way of life.

These Islamists – we must get used to this word, "Islamists," meaning those who are engaged upon such political projects, and learn to distinguish it from the more general and politically neutral "Muslim" – include the Muslim Brotherhood in Egypt, the blood-soaked combatants of the Islamic Salvation Front and Armed Islamic Group in Algeria, the Shiite revolutionaries of Iran, and the Taliban. Poverty is their great helper, and the fruit of their efforts is paranoia. This paranoid Islam, which blames outsiders, "infidels," for all the ills of Muslim societies, and whose proposed remedy is the closing of those societies to the rival project of modernity, is presently the fastest growing version of Islam in the world.[27]

---

27 www.nytimes.com/2001/11/02/opinion/yes-this-is-about-islam.html

CHAPTER TWENTY-SIX

Is the Jihad Really the Core of Islamic Doctrine?

Let's read what the Koran, the Islamic Holy Scriptures, says:

> And those who perform jihad for Us, We shall certainly guide them in our ways, and God is surely with the doers of good.
>
> Sura 29:69

> O you who believe! Shall I guide you to a commerce that will save you from a painful torment? That you believe in Allah and His Messenger and that you strive hard and fight in the Cause of Allah with your wealth and your lives, that will be better for you, if you but know! (If you do so) He will forgive you your sins, and admit you into Gardens under which rivers flow, and pleasant dwelling

in Gardens of Eternity, that is indeed the great success.

Sura 61:10-12

O you who believe! Do not take the Jews and the Christians for friends; they are friends of each other; and whoever amongst you takes them for a friend, then surely he is one of them; surely Allah does not guide the unjust people. Your friend can be only Allah; and His messenger and those who believe.

O you who believe! Do not take for guardians those who take your religion for a mockery and a joke, from among those who were given the Book before you and the unbelievers; and be careful of (your duty to) Allah if you are believers.

Sura 5:51, 57

The punishment of those who wage war against Allah and His Apostle and strive to make mischief in the land is only this, that they should be murdered or crucified or their hands and their feet should be cut off on opposite sides or they should be imprisoned; this shall be as a disgrace for them in this world, and in the hereafter they shall have a grievous chastisement.

Sura 5:33

So when the sacred months have passed away, then slay the idolaters wherever you find them, and take

IS THE JIHAD REALLY THE CORE OF ISLAMIC DOCTRINE?

them captives and besiege them and lie in wait for them in every ambush, then if they repent and keep up prayer and pay the poor-rate, leave their way free to them; surely Allah is forgiving, Merciful.

Sura 9:5

O Prophet! Strive hard against the unbelievers and the hypocrites and be unyielding to them; and their abode is hell, and evil is the destination.

Sura 9:73

O you who believe! Fight those of the unbelievers who are near to you and let them find you in hardness; and know that Allah is with those who guard (against evil).

Sura 9:123

And fight with them until there is no more persecution and religion should be only for Allah, but if they desist, then surely Allah sees what they do."

Sura 8:39

You shall prepare for them all the power you can muster, and all the equipment you can mobilize, that you may frighten the enemies of GOD, your enemies, as well as others who are not known to you; GOD knows them. Whatever you spend in the cause of GOD will be repaid to you generously, without the least injustice. If they resort to peace, so shall you, and put your trust in GOD. He is the Hearer, the Omniscient."

Sura 8:60-61

Could it be any clearer than that? Islam is condemned by its own words, its own scriptures, and its own actions of evil.

What Does the Hadith Say About Jihad?

The Prophet said, "The person who participates in [Holy battles] in Allah's cause and nothing compels him to do so except belief in Allah and His Apostles, will be recompensed by Allah either with a reward, or booty (if he survives) or will be admitted to Paradise (if he is killed in the battle as a martyr). Had I not found it difficult for my followers, then I would not remain behind any sariya going for Jihad and I would have loved to be martyred in Allah's cause and then made alive, and then martyred and then made alive, and then again martyred in His cause."

Vol.1, Book 2, Number 35.
Narrated by Abu Huraira.

Allah's Apostle said, "A pious slave gets a double reward." Abu Huraira added: By Him in Whose Hands my soul is but for Jihad (i.e. holy battles),

Hajj, and my duty to serve my mother, I would have loved to die as a slave."
Volume 3, Book 46, Number 724.
Narrated by Abu Huraira.

Allah's Apostle said, "Allah guarantees him who strives in His Cause and whose motivation for going out is nothing but Jihad in His Cause and belief in His Word, that He will admit him into Paradise (if martyred) or bring him back to his dwelling place, whence he has come out, with what he gains of reward and booty."
Volume 9, Book 93, Number 555.
Narrated by Abu Huraira.

The Doctrine of the Hijrah

We are seeing a massive population redistribution occurring at an alarming rate across the globe.

Hijrah. Learn the word. Understand it and never forget it. Because Hijrah accurately describes the mass migration scenario unfolding in Europe, and now, in America.

In the year 622, the Islamic prophet Muhammad set out on the first Hijrah. What is a Hijrah? In short, it's the act of migrating to other parts of the world with the intention of spreading the grip of Islam.

From the Quran:

> And whoever emigrates for the cause of Allah will find on the earth many locations and abundance. And whoever leaves his home as an emigrant to Allah and His Messenger and then death overtakes him, his reward has already become incumbent upon Allah. And Allah is ever Forgiving and Merciful.
>
> Quran 4:100

The Middle East represents the fastest-growing bloc of immigrants admitted into the country on visas, according to a census-databased report by the Center for Immigration Studies. Student visas for Middle Eastern countries have similarly accelerated enormously, including sixteen-fold increase in Saudi students since 9/11. Arabic is the most common language among refugees, and over 90% of recent refugees from the Middle East are on food stamps.

Mass Migration is so important that the Islamic calendar is based upon the doctrine of the Hijrah, Mohammed's migration from Mecca to Medina. Why? Because it was this mass migration that brought about the doctrine of jihad.

And it was these two doctrines – Hijrah and jihad – that made Islam triumphant. It conquered its neighbors by population invasion. It demanded conversion or death for the inhabitants of every country they spilled into.

The raging Muslim hordes massacred millions of native populations. An entire village would be brought out into the main square, and the men of the village would be beheaded, and the women raped and left for dead.

IS THE JIHAD REALLY THE CORE OF ISLAMIC DOCTRINE?

The next villages were quick to bow to Allah, and yet the slaughter continued. They killed wantonly like madmen. Their swords fell forever in action. That is why you see the sword so prominent on most Muslim flags.

Moving masses of Muslims into areas where they soon take over control – by butchering, raping, tormenting, and torturing the native population – has been the key to its growth throughout the Mid-East. Now it is overwhelming Europe, and beginning in the United States.

ISIS openly boasted that they have sent over two thousand terrorists into Europe during this present invasion. The horror of the Friday the 13th massacres in Paris was just the start of it. America is next.

What we see in the mass Muslim invasions into Europe, and in the hundreds of thousands of unvetted Muslims in the United States, are the uncountable numbers of terrorists among them, placed to kill and destroy. It isn't what *we* say. It is what *they* say.

CHAPTER TWENTY-SEVEN
Beyond the Jihad: Apocalyptic Islam

Many people are aware that the Bible carries a detailed eschatology – or End Times theology – as outlined in books like Daniel and Revelation. They can at least quote such topics as Armageddon or the Four Horsemen of the Apocalypse. But what seems less known is that Islam carries its own apocalyptic theology and prophecies, which serve as part of the impetus for their acts of terror. Let me quote from an exceptional study by author Joel Rosenberg in the matter of the end times from the Muslim viewpoint.

> There is a dramatic shift underway in the Muslim world. The most serious threat we face in the Middle East and North Africa is no longer radical Islam, but apocalyptic Islam. We face not just one, but two regional regimes, whose rulers are driven not merely by violent political ideology or extremist theology, but by apocalyptic, genocidal eschatology,

or End Times theology. The first is the Islamic Republic of Iran. The second is the Islamic State, or ISIS. The leaders of the former are Shia; the latter are Sunni.

Both believe that we are living in the End of Days as predicted in their ancient prophecies. Both believe that any moment now their messiah, the Mahdi, will be revealed on Earth as he establishes his global Islamic kingdom and imposes sharia law. Both believe that Jesus will return, not as the Savior or Son of God, but as a lieutenant to the Mahdi, and that he will force non-Muslims to convert or die. What's more, both believe that the Mahdi will come only when the world is engulfed in chaos and carnage.

They openly vow not simply to attack, but to annihilate the United States and Israel. Iran and ISIS are both eager to hasten the coming of the Mahdi. Both believe that the Day of Judgment is coming soon, when they will be either rewarded for their actions, or condemned to hell for eternity. And both are receiving relatively minimal international opposition. Consequently, both believe that Allah is on their side, that the wind is at their back, and that victory is both assured and imminent. [28]

---

28 Joel C. Rosenberg, September 11, 2015. www.nationalreview.com/article/423852/islamic-extremists-are-trying-hasten-coming-mahdi-joel-c-rosenberg

CHAPTER TWENTY-EIGHT
The Glory of Martyrdom – A Holy Death

The Islamic Jihad recruits young Muslims by means of religious indoctrination, and bases its terrorist strategy on the willingness of these young people to lay down their lives for what they see as a divine command: the war against the infidels.

Many of the Jihad's terrorist attacks are designed as suicide operations in which the terrorist attempts to cause as many casualties as possible, without planning his own escape. That approach certainly makes it difficult to anticipate and turn aside from these attacks.

These young men, and some women as well, are taken captive by the rhetoric and fanaticism of their religious leaders and the complacency of their governments, who either agree with this barbaric level of religious zeal or stand to the side out of fear of angering them.

With the availability of the internet, and the glorification of martyrdom, recruits from across the world are flooding into places like Syria to fight against the infidels, while at the same time, hundreds of thousands of like-minded young men pour into Europe, and now the United States, to fight and destroy us, the enemy in our own cities and towns.

It is sad to see many places in Europe and the United States taken over by Islamification and sharia law. In some cities even the police do not enter because of the violent nature of the Muslims living there.

CHAPTER TWENTY-NINE
The Words of Winston Churchill

In September 1898, twenty-three-year-old Winston Churchill was one of the officers leading the 21st Lancers cavalry charge that secured a British victory over nineteenth century Islamic terrorists at the Battle of Omdurman in Sudan.

In *The River War,* his account of the British retaking of Sudan, published in 1899, Churchill noted the threat to Western Civilization posed by radical Islam:

> Individual Moslems may show splendid qualities. Thousands become the brave and loyal soldiers of the Queen: all know how to die: but the influence of the religion paralyzes the social development of those who follow it. **No stronger retrograde force exists in the world.** Far from being moribund, Mohammedanism is a militant and proselytising faith. It has already spread throughout Central Africa, raising fearless warriors at every step; and

were it not that Christianity is sheltered in the strong arms of science—the science against which it had vainly struggled—the civilisation of modern Europe might fall, as fell the civilisation of ancient Rome.

How dreadful are the curses which Mohammedanism lays on its votaries! Besides the fanatical frenzy, which is as dangerous in a man as hydrophobia in a dog, there is this fearful, fatalistic apathy. The effects are apparent in many countries. Improvident habits, slovenly systems of agriculture, sluggish methods of commerce, and insecurity of property exist wherever the followers of the Prophet rule or live. A degraded sensualism deprives this life of its grace and refinement; the next of its dignity and sanctity. The fact that in Mohammedanism law every woman must belong to some man as his absolute property – either as a child, a wife, or a concubine – must delay the final extinction of slavery until the faith of Islam has ceased to be a great power among men.[29]

---

29 www.breitbart.com/big-government/2015/12/28/century-donald-trump-churchill-warned-no-stronger-retrograde-force-exists-world-islam/

CHAPTER THIRTY
Finally, Brethren, Some Words of Sound Advice

And whereas it is the duty of nations as well as of men, to own their dependence upon the overruling power of God, to confess their sins and transgressions, in humble sorrow, yet with assured hope that genuine repentance will lead to mercy and pardon; and to recognize the sublime truth, announced in the Holy Scriptures and proven by all history, that those nations only are blessed whose God is the Lord.

And, insomuch as we know that, by His divine law, nations like individuals are subjected to punishments and chastisements in this world, may we not justly fear that the awful calamity of civil war, which now desolates the land, may be but a punishment, inflicted upon us, for our presumptuous sins, to the needful end of our national reformation as a whole People?

We have been the recipients of the choicest bounties of Heaven. We have been preserved, these many years, in peace and prosperity. We have grown in numbers, wealth and power, as no other nation has ever grown.

But we have forgotten God.

We have forgotten the gracious hand that preserved us in peace, and multiplied and enriched and strengthened us; and we have vainly imagined, in the deceitfulness of our hearts, that all these blessings were produced by some superior wisdom and virtue of our own. Intoxicated with unbroken success, we have become too self-sufficient to feel the necessity of redeeming and preserving grace, too proud to pray to the God that made us!

It behooves us then, to humble ourselves before the offended Power, to confess our national sins, and to pray for clemency and forgiveness.

Abraham Lincoln, March 30, 1863.

CHAPTER THIRTY-ONE

Witnessing to Muslims

Muslims may be the most difficult people group in the world in their willingness to accept a witness of your Christian belief.

Previously, I mentioned that if just a tenth of a tenth of a tenth of all Muslims fall into the category of violent Jihadists, there would still be millions of Muslims ready to kill for Allah.

Likewise, I believe that if just a tenth of a tenth of all the Muslims in America would be open to hearing the good news of the Gospel, we need to be prepared to offer it.

Unfortunately, I have been approached by those Muslims who simply want to argue doctrine, and I have to tell you that, at best, it is a futile effort.

This is a mission field of prayer, fasting, and displaying true Christian character in daily lifestyle evangelism. You need to be ready when that one Muslim is ready to listen, and you need to know how and when, if ever, to share.

This is one time when you really need to be listening to the Holy Spirit.

With a people group buried alive in the spiritual darkness of Islam and sharia law, most with a minimal education, the key must be what is right about your way of life, and not what is wrong with theirs.

Let me share some things from a witnessing website that I believe represents what I am trying to say:

Reaching Muslims for Christ is a Process[30]

Start from the understanding that it will be a long process, and will be frustrating at times.

Why? Because witnessing to them is only in a small part about theology. A Muslim's decision to accept Jesus Christ is 10% theology based and 90% community based (Umma).

When you witness to a Muslim about Jesus Christ, your theology is the truth, and most will admit they know it is the truth, but they are extremely fearful about leaving the community of their upbringing.

If you have accepted Jesus Christ as your savior, and know it was by grace, then your theology is miles ahead of anything that most Muslims know. But, you cannot easily replace the community to which they all belong.

---

[30] www.centerformissions.com

Islam means peace?

There is some idea that Islam translates as the word "peace" in English.

That is not correct. Islam means *submission*. So a Muslim is one who strives to submit to God.

Muslims are essentially fatalists. Everything that happens, no matter how big or small, is God's will. *En Shalla* is a phrase commonly used by Arab Muslims. It means, "If God wills it."

A works-based faith

Islam is a works-based faith. Apologist C.S. Lewis said, "Islam is the ultimate [works] heresy of Christianity."

So a Muslim is one who must continue to follow the five "pillars of Islam" and continually try to do good works. The five pillars are:

- **Confession of Faith.** "There is no God but Allah and Mohammed is the prophet of God."

- **Prayer.** Muslims are supposed to pray five times a day: shortly before sunrise, mid-morning, noon, mid-afternoon, and after sunset.

- **Give alms.** Muslims are to give about 2.5% of their wealth – Zacat or Tacat.

- **Fast during Ramadan.** For one lunar month, from sunrise to sunset, Muslims are not to allow anything to pass down their throat. (Theoretically, a good Muslim would even spit out his or her saliva.) Then from sunset to sunrise, they are permitted to eat as little or as much as they want.

This is their way of developing discipline and relating to the poor. (Travelers, young children, and pregnant or nursing mothers do not need to keep the fast.)

- **Make a pilgrimage to Mecca.** Every Muslim who is financially able is supposed to travel to the birthplace of Islam once in his or her lifetime.

You catch more bees with honey than vinegar

Most Muslims will be interested in knowing more about Christianity. In some cases they may want to witness to you about Islam. In some cases they are just curious.

They all have a lot of false information about Christianity. Their only reference is television and the orthodox worship they see to some extent in their native countries.

You can use the five pillars to make a connection to a Muslim in witnessing. If the five pillars are brought up, or if you ask them to tell you about them, here is a way you can start your discussion using them as the basis:

- **Confession of Faith.** "As a Christian I believe what the Torah says, "hear O Israel, The LORD our God, the LORD is one" (Deuteronomy 6:4).

- **Prayer.** "As a Christian I believe what is written in the Injeel (Gopsels)," that we are to "pray without ceasing" (1 Thessalonians 5:17).

- **Give Alms.** "As a Christian I believe what is written in the Injeel (Gospels), that we are to "reach out to the homeless and widows" (James 1:27).

- **Fasting.** "As a Christian I believe in fasting. We do not have a public time for it, and consider it a private matter between God and us" (Matthew 6:16-18).

- **Pilgrimage.** "As a Christian we believe God is present everywhere, but it can be enriching to our faith if we can visit the places where our faith began.
  "But, as a Christian I do not believe that my salvation is based on those practices. I am certain of my salvation because God promised to save me by His grace."

Grace versus mercy

Islam is a faith of uncertainty. Allah is "capricious," and can at his whim accept the Muslim to paradise or send them to hell. They rely on the "mercy" of Allah. There is no certainty of paradise in Islam, except through Jihad.

Your assurance of salvation will attract their interest.

Jihad does not *necessarily* mean what we have come to think of from the 9/11 attacks against nonbelievers.

Technically, the Muslim is participating in Jihad if they are "forcefully promoting Islam." It may be proselytizing, or even just speaking publicly about the faith. It may be them inviting you to see the mosque or to celebrate the Iftar (breaking of the fast in Ramadan) with you.

Your encounter with a Muslim

If you believe you are called by God to witness to Muslims, then you need more information and study than is provided here.

However, if you want to be prepared to share a witness to a Muslim when the opportunity presents itself, then what is provided here is probably adequate.

If you want to argue over theology or the pedigree of the Prophet Mohammed, then you should rethink witnessing to Muslims.

When you encounter a Muslim:

- Pray for the Holy Spirit to direct you and your conversations. Just a quick, whispered word is okay.

- Be courteous and loving. Outside of the close family unit, and in particular outside of the community (umma), most Muslims do not have close friends.

- If you use the name Mohammed, be sure to refer to him as "the prophet Mohammed" or just "the prophet." No religious Muslim will say his name without a blessing on him.

- Show an interest in their beliefs. Allow them time to articulate their views.

- Become acquainted with their basic beliefs, but unless you really want to know everything, it is not important to read the Koran and the Hadith.

- If they suggest or want you to read the Koran, ask them to get you a copy in English and ask if you can give them a copy of the Bible in English and their heart language (it may not be Arabic). The Koran says it is okay to read the Torah (the first five books of the Hebrew Bible), the Zabur (Psalms), and the Injeel (Gospels).

- Ask lots of questions about Islam. You will probably discover they do not know a lot of answers for your questions.

- Ask them if they would like to know what you believe.

- Be willing to examine passages of the Koran concerning their beliefs. You don't have to respond.

- Stick to the cardinal doctrines of the Christian faith, but also take time to respond to all sincere questions.

  1. Point out the centrality of the person and work of Jesus Christ for salvation.

  2. Stress that because of Jesus, His cross, and resurrection, one may have the full assurance of salvation, both now and for eternity (see 1 John 5:13).

  3. Share the plan of salvation with the Muslim. Point out that salvation is a gift and not to be earned.

  4. Be willing to become a friend and involve them in community, "your umma," or introduce them to a community of saved Muslims.

The "trap" questions

You may be asked questions that will become a "trap" unless you are prepared to give them an answer.

They will be expecting your answer to be one that rejects them, their prophet, and their faith. The questions may go something like this:

"What do you think of Islam?"

"What do you think of the Prophet Mohammed?"

"Why does the U.S. government support Israel (Palestine) and allow them to kill the Palestinians?"

The goal in answering these questions well is to find some common ground to allow you to continue your witness and generate some curiosity in them about what you just told them without compromising your faith.

Here are a few facts about Islam – although we won't really agree with them completely in our response – that you can use to provide an answer to these types of questions and keep the door open.

- Muslims believe in one true God, whose name in Arabic is Allah.

- Muslims believe in angels, both good and bad.

- Muslims believe that God revealed His word to men and women in certain "books."

- Muslims believe in God's many prophets – including Adam, Abraham, Moses.

- Muslims believe that there will be a second coming of Jesus that will usher in a last day of judgment.

- Muslims believe that Jesus was born of a virgin named Mary.

- Muslims believe that God is involved in human affairs.

- Muslims believe in life after death.

So here are some ideas regarding how to answer those types of questions that will allow you to tell the truth, but still have an opportunity to continue the dialogue with them.

"What do you think of the prophet Mohammed?"

"The prophet Mohammed wanted to restore the worship of the one true God. As a Christian, I share that desire."

What do you think of Muslims?

"Muslims believe God revealed Himself in the Torah, the Psalms and the Gospels. As a Christian, I share that belief.

"Muslims believe that Jesus will return and usher in a time of final judgment for which all men and women need to be prepared. As a Christian, I share that belief."

What do you think of the Koran?

"I'm sure it must be an interesting book, but as a Christian I do not see how it adds to the other revelations Muslims accept – the Torah, the Psalms, and the Gospels."

Why does the U.S. government support Israel and allow them to kill Palestinians?
"I am not representing the U.S. government. I just wanted to find out more about you and your faith."

Finally, *be sure to ask them if there is anything you can pray for them about.*

In particular, mention that you will have your church begin praying for them in whatever matter they bring up. Write it down, and do what you told them. Most Muslims will be shocked that you will do that.

Be sure to follow up with them and don't hesitate to invite them to your church activities.

Finally, remember that it is the Holy Spirit that convicts and draws them to Jesus. Let Him work.

CHAPTER THIRTY-TWO

A Call to Arms

I love that great old hymn that goes like this:

> *Onward, Christian soldiers, marching as to war,*
> *   with the cross of Jesus going on before.*
> *Christ, the royal Master, leads against the foe;*
> *   forward into battle see his banners go!*
> *Onward, Christian soldiers, marching as to war,*
> *   with the cross of Jesus going on before.*
> *At the sign of triumph Satan's host doth flee;*
> *   on then, Christian soldiers, on to victory!*
> *Hell's foundations quiver at the shout of praise;*
> *   brothers, lift your voices, loud your anthems raise.*

Let's praise the Lord we are here in such a time of need, a time to be that hand extended, that ambassador in bonds, that one sent forth to be the representative of Christ Jesus. Let our every prayer, our every action, be one that would please Him. Pray longer, deeper, and with all your prayers, supplications, and actions, glorify Him.

Lest we forget – America must remain America!

God bless our country and our heroes.

Portions of this book have been taken from earlier publications by Ed Decker, including *Understanding Islam: The Mystery Religion*, published by Lamp Post Publishers, 2011, and from *Fast Facts of False Teachings*, coauthored with Dr. Ron Carlson, Harvest House Publishing, 1994.

Ed Decker
P.O. Box 1347, Issaquah WA 98027
www.saintsalive.com
ed@saintsalive.com

www.ingramcontent.com/pod-product-compliance
Lightning Source LLC
Chambersburg PA
CBHW030524080526
44586CB00011B/314